The CHEW

QUICK & EASY

STRESS-FREE RECIPES FOR EVERY OCCASION

ALSO AVAILABLE FROM *THE CHEW*

The *New York Times* best-selling books:
The Chew: Food. Life. Fun.
The Chew: What's for Dinner?
The Chew: A Year of Celebrations
The Chew: An Essential Guide to Cooking and Entertaining
The Chew Approved

The CHEW

QUICK & EASY

STRESS-FREE RECIPES FOR EVERY OCCASION

Edited by Ashley Archer

KINGSWELL

LOS ANGELES • NEW YORK

PAGE 2: **Affogato Milk Shake** courtesy of Mario Batali, recipe on page 202.

PAGE 6: **Stuffed Shells with Corn and Zucchini** courtesy of Michael Symon, recipe on page 126.

Content Coordinator: Janet Arvelo
Researcher: Giselle Snyder
Food Photographer: Andrew Scrivani
Senior Food Stylist: Jackie Rothong
Food Stylist: Alexandra Utter
Prop Stylist: Soo-Jeong Kang
Junior Food Stylist: Kelly Janke
Assistant Food Stylist: Michele Figliuolo

Cover Host Photographer: Craig Sjodin/ABC

Photographer credits:
Heidi Gutman: 5; Lou Rocco: 10-11, 18, 20, 41, 55, 90, 124, 136-137, 146, 191, 221, 228; Lorenzo Bevilaqua: 22-23, 39, 50, 59, 68, 72, 74-75, 82, 84-85, 99, 101, 116, 120-121, 130, 140, 149, 152, 158-159, 160, 164, 169, 170-171, 186-187, 195, 204-205, 210-211, 212, 218-219, 223, 239, 243, 244-245; Jeff Neira: 8-9, 30, 37, 44, 60, 79, 80, 92-93, 94, 96, 104, 106, 108-109, 115, 176, 182, 192, 200, 230; Ida Mae Astute: 34-35, 206; Paula Lobo: 42-43, 113, 128-129, 144-145, 178-179, 216, 226-227; Fred Lee: 48-49, 64, 66-67, 71, 155, 170-171, 234-235

For information address Kingswell, 1101 Flower Street, Glendale, California 91201.

Editorial Director: Wendy Lefkon
Executive Editor: Laura Hopper
Designer: Gregory Wakabayashi / Welcome Enterprises, Inc., New York

ISBN 978-1-368-00791-7
FAC-008598-17223

FIRST PAPERBACK EDITION, SEPTEMBER 2017
10 9 8 7 6 5 4 3 2 1

SUSTAINABLE FORESTRY INITIATIVE — Certified Sourcing
www.sfiprogram.org
SFI-00993
Logo Applies to Text Stock Only

CONTENTS

Introduction

After answering thousands of your questions not only on our show but on every social media platform known to Silicon Valley, we think we have a pretty good idea of what you need most from us here at *The Chew*. It's almost unanimous: in a million different ways and in a million different voices: you are screaming for Quick & Easy meals!

In fact, you've asked us for the most delicious meals we have ever created using the fewest ingredients possible. These are meals that will take up the least amount of your oh-so-precious time. You've asked for meals that have fewer items, so you can stay out of crazy long checkout lines and instead to cruise right through the express lane.

We know you also want meals that leave little or nothing to clean up afterward, superfast dishes to entertain your friends and family, and dinners you can whip up on the fly with ingredients that are probably already in your fridge. Oh, and last but not least, we've added recipes for incredibly easy desserts to satisfy any sweet tooth.

Well, it's a tall order, but here at *The Chew*, our hosts love a challenge. So, we've narrowed it down to our absolute favorites, and after going through each recipe, we think we've covered all of your requests. We're giving you recipes that will be a hit and help you navigate through even the darkest of dining dilemmas.

Like any great dish, it's what we left out that makes this book so good.

Enjoy!

—Gordon Elliott

Chapter 1

10 Ingredients or Less

Here at *The Chew* we want you to know that we really try our hardest to give you the tools that you need to be successful in the kitchen. I always go back to one idea, whether I'm cooking for two or two hundred, and that's *Keep it simple*! Why make a ton of work for yourself when you can create a delicious meal with just a few key ingredients?

We've all been there, looking through our favorite cookbooks for some inspiration, stopping at a beautiful photo or an interesting-sounding title, only to find that to make the dish you need twenty-five ingredients, most of which you can't even pronounce. And when that recipe calls for some obscure tool or cooking device that you've never heard of, there's just nothing left to do but give up and order takeout. It happens to the best of us.

Well, not anymore! In this chapter, we've got simple recipes that are easy to put together but still have that wow factor that keeps your family and friends coming back for more. We've got amazing appetizers, elegant entrées, holiday shortcuts, and lots of game-day grub to keep things interesting. And each of these delightful dishes uses fewer than ten ingredients, many of which you've probably got in your fridge or pantry right now.

I guess the hard part is choosing which one of these delectable dinners to make tonight!

—CARLA HALL

French Toast Roll-Up

Serves: 4 / **Prep Time:** 10 minutes / **Cook Time:** 5 minutes

Courtesy of Clinton Kelly / Imagine this: The day is new, you're swaddled in the sheets with a little sleep still left in your eyes, and the birds are chirping outside. It's a beautiful day and you're feeling great, and then . . . the phone rings. Your family wants to stop by for brunch to catch up, kids and all. Well, don't fret, because I've got a really easy dish for you that will impress every single one of those unexpected guests and have the entire family wondering how you became such a fantastic host. So get back under those covers and relax; you've got plenty of time to whip up these sweet little rolls before company arrives.

2 large eggs

¼ cup milk

1 tablespoon cinnamon

¼ cup sugar

8 slices white bread, crusts cut off

1 cup chocolate hazelnut spread

1 banana, peeled, cut in half widthwise, then quartered lengthwise

2 tablespoons butter, plus more if needed

1. In a shallow dish, whisk the eggs and milk together. In a separate shallow dish, combine the cinnamon and the sugar, and set aside.

2. Using a rolling pin, roll out each slice of bread until about ⅛-inch thick. Cover each slice with the chocolate hazelnut spread and one slice of the banana. Roll the bread up tightly like a sushi roll. Dip each of the roll-ups in the egg mixture.

3. Place a nonstick sauté pan over medium heat, add the butter, and allow to melt. Place the roll-ups in the sauté pan and allow to cook for 1–2 minutes per side, until golden brown. Remove to a serving platter and sprinkle generously with the cinnamon-sugar mixture. Serve warm.

Chilaquiles

Serves: 6 / **Prep Time:** 5 minutes / **Cook Time:** 10 minutes

Courtesy of Mario Batali / I am a huge fan of Mexican cuisine. The flavors are really bright and bold, and as my cohosts will tell you, I love spicy food. This dish is a classic at our brunch table on the weekends and is a great way to use up all of those broken corn tortillas that you have left in the bottom of the bag. Traditionally, chilaquiles is served with either red or green salsa. I prefer the fresh tangy flavor of the green tomatillo salsa, but feel free to play around with whatever kind of sauce you like. Gather all of your ingredients together before you start cooking, because this dish comes together super quick. And it's eaten even quicker.

4 tablespoons extra-virgin olive oil

6 corn tortillas

4 tablespoons unsalted butter

6 large eggs, lightly beaten

2 cups store-bought roasted tomatillo salsa

Kosher salt and freshly ground black pepper, to taste

1½ cups white cheddar cheese, grated

½ cup sour cream

4 tablespoons fresh cilantro leaves, chopped

Lime wedges, for garnish

1. Place a 10-inch nonstick pan over medium-high heat. Heat the oil until it starts to shimmer. Cut the tortillas into 8 pieces each, like a pie. Toss the tortilla pieces into the oil and cook until crisp, stirring constantly. Remove pieces to a paper towel to drain.

2. Reduce heat to medium. Add butter to pan and swirl until light golden brown. Add the eggs and the tomatillo salsa, season with salt and pepper, and cook slowly, stirring constantly with a whisk, until soft curds form. Add the cooked tortillas and half of the cheese and stir through until just set.

3. To serve, place some of the eggs on each plate and then add 2 tablespoons of the cheddar cheese. Top with a dollop of the sour cream and garnish each serving with a tablespoon of the chopped cilantro leaves and a lime wedge.

Coddled Eggs with Spinach and Goat Cheese

Serves: 4 / Prep Time: 15 minutes / **Cook Time:** 15 minutes

Courtesy of Clinton Kelly / These perfectly cooked eggs are a great dish to serve at a luncheon or even a baby shower, because you can assemble the cups the night before everyone arrives and cook them in batches. Choose two or three of your favorite flavor combinations. Set them out on the table with little place cards marked with the ingredients so that guests can choose which cup they would like to eat. These work really well in a buffet-style setting and add a nice festive feel to any gathering. Try serving them with some toast points and a light salad.

2 tablespoons butter

4 ounces baby spinach

Kosher salt and freshly ground black pepper, to taste

1 store-bought roasted red pepper, diced

¼ cup goat cheese, crumbled

8 large eggs

½ cup heavy cream, divided

1 tablespoon chives, finely chopped

8 slices white bread, toasted and cut in half on an angle

1. Preheat oven to 325°F.

2. Heat a large sauté pan over medium heat and add 1 tablespoon of butter. Once butter is melted, add spinach and season with salt and pepper. Sauté just until the spinach has wilted. Remove from heat.

3. Line the bottom of a 9 x 9 baking dish with a clean kitchen towel. Fill pan with 1 inch of hot water.

4. Meanwhile, grease the inside of 4 8-ounce ramekins with 1 tablespoon of butter. Divide sautéed spinach among the ramekins. Top each with some roasted pepper, goat cheese, 2 eggs, and 2 tablespoons of cream. Season with salt and pepper.

5. Place ramekins in baking dish and cover first with a piece of parchment and then with a piece of foil. Bake 10–12 minutes, until whites are set and yolks are still runny.

6. Carefully remove ramekins from baking dish. Serve on 4 plates lined with a napkin. Garnish with chives. Serve with toast if you'd like.

Curry Chicken Salad

Serves: 6–8 / **Prep Time:** 20 minutes / **Cook Time:** 30 minutes

Courtesy of Carla Hall / You know that I'm always talking about being a recovering caterer. Back in the day when I used to cater parties for hundreds of people at a time, this dish was a staple on my menu. It's a huge crowd-pleaser and it takes no time to put together. I've simplified my recipe a little and swapped out store-bought rotisserie chicken for the labor-intensive poached version, which saves you even more time. Whether served in lettuce cups or endive leaves, or on potato rolls or as a tea sandwich, it's the perfect passed appetizer or light lunch for any occasion.

2 tablespoons extra-virgin olive oil

1 small onion, peeled and finely chopped

2 tablespoons curry powder

1½ cups mayonnaise

¾ cup mango, peeled and diced

1 lime, zested and juiced

Kosher salt, to taste

1 rotisserie chicken (skin and bones discarded), shredded

¼ cup cilantro, roughly chopped

½ cup cashews, toasted, roughly chopped

1. In a large sauté pan, add the olive oil over medium heat. Add onion and sauté until almost tender, about 5 minutes. Add the curry powder and cook an additional 2 minutes. Remove to a bowl and allow to cool completely.

2. In a large bowl add the mayonnaise, mango, lime juice and zest, and onion mixture, and season with salt. Add the rotisserie chicken, cilantro, and cashews, and mix until just combined. Taste for seasoning and serve.

Lightened-Up Chicken Reuben

Serves: 4 / **Prep Time:** 15 minutes / **Cook Time:** 15 minutes

Courtesy of Clinton Kelly / A Reuben, piled high with pastrami and creamy coleslaw, sandwiched between two slices of rye bread, is one of my favorite diner delights. If I could eat this perfect sandwich all the time, believe me I would! But one of these deli-style sandwiches can pile on upwards of a thousand calories! When I heard that, I swore them off for good. And then the cravings settled in, and well, you know the drill. So I developed this low-cal version that tastes every bit as delicious as the real deal, though I can feel good about eating it. At about half the calories of the traditional Reuben, you can eat this slammin' sandwich as often as you want.

4 boneless, skinless chicken thighs

Kosher salt and freshly ground black pepper, to taste

4 slices dark rye bread, lightly toasted

4 slices Swiss cheese

FOR THE NAPA CABBAGE COLESLAW:

1 medium head Napa cabbage, shredded

1 jalapeño, seeded, thinly sliced

2 teaspoons celery seed

2 teaspoons mayonnaise

2 tablespoons ketchup

2 teaspoons sweet pickle relish

1. Preheat outdoor grill or greased grill pan to medium heat.

2. Preheat broiler in oven. Place oven rack at the top of the oven.

3. Season chicken thighs with salt and pepper. Place on preheated grill. Grill for 4–5 minutes per side, or until the internal temperature reaches 165°F. Remove from grill, let rest for 5 minutes. Slice chicken thighs into 5 pieces per chicken thigh.

4. Lay slices of toasted dark rye bread on a baking sheet. Add the sliced chicken and top with slaw and a slice of Swiss cheese. Place under broiler for 1–2 minutes, until cheese has melted.

FOR THE NAPA CABBAGE COLESLAW:

5. In a large bowl, add the Napa cabbage, jalapeño, and celery seed. Toss to combine. In a small bowl, add mayonnaise, ketchup, and relish, and whisk to combine. Drizzle over Napa cabbage mixture and toss to combine. Season with salt and pepper.

Swiss Chard and Ricotta Pizza Poppers

Makes: 24 pockets / **Prep Time:** 20–25 minutes / **Cook Time:** 15 minutes

Courtesy of Carla Hall / This dish is a really fun twist on the classic delivery-style pizza, and I think it's great for a game-day appetizer. Kids and adults both love it, so feel free to play around with your favorite pizza toppings. Just fry up that store-bought pizza dough that you can pick up at your local pizzeria or find in the freezer section of your grocery store, then stuff it with whatever you've got hanging out in your fridge: mozzarella and pepperoni, Swiss chard and ricotta, ham and cheddar. Seriously, you can't go wrong with these decadent little pizza bites.

4 cups, plus 2 tablespoons vegetable oil

2 cloves garlic, peeled and thinly sliced

1 bunch Swiss chard, ribs removed and finely chopped

1 teaspoon red pepper flakes

Kosher salt and freshly ground black pepper, to taste

3 cups ricotta, drained

¼ cup freshly grated Parmigiano-Reggiano

¼ cup extra-virgin olive oil

1 pound store-bought pizza dough

2 cups store-bought tomato sauce

1. Fill a large cast iron skillet halfway up the sides with vegetable oil and place over medium heat until a thermometer reads 350°F.

2. Heat a large sauté pan with 2 tablespoons vegetable oil over medium-high heat. Add garlic and cook until fragrant. Sauté Swiss chard for about 5–7 minutes, until wilted. Season with red pepper flakes, salt, and pepper. Remove from heat to a bowl and allow to cool.

3. Once at room temperature, stir in ricotta, Parmigiano-Reggiano, and olive oil. Season to taste with salt and pepper. Place filling in a piping bag fitted with a pastry tube that is about 3¾ inches long and about ¼-inch wide.

4. Dust a large work surface with flour. If the dough has been refrigerated, transfer to the work surface and let stand just until still cool but not cold.

5. Roll out dough to about ¼-inch thickness. Using a 2-inch cookie cutter, begin cutting out 2-inch circles.

6. Drop the 2-inch-round circles of pizza dough into the oil. Fry for 4–5 minutes until dough puffs up and is golden brown on both sides. Remove to a paper towel–lined plate. Once cool enough to handle, begin piping each pizza pocket with filling. Pierce both sides of the puff with a paring knife or pastry tube tip and fill. Serve immediately with a side of your favorite tomato sauce for dipping.

Mozzarella Sticks

Makes: 15 sticks / **Prep Time:** 15 minutes / **Cook Time:** 10 minutes

Courtesy of Clinton Kelly / You may not eat mozzarella sticks anymore, but I know you did as a kid, and I know that you secretly love them. I mean, who doesn't get a craving every once in a while for hot stringy cheese breaded and deep-fried? I know I do. This recipe is great because I take that classic mozzarella cheese and wrap it in wonton skins, fold them up into neat little packages, and sauté them in a little bit of oil. That's right, they're not deep-fried, which is a huge plus for two reasons: there's no oil to clean up, and there are fewer calories to work off at the gym. It's a win-win, people.

15 square egg roll wrappers

1 pound low-moisture mozzarella cheese, cut into ½-inch x 4-inch logs

Kosher salt and freshly ground black pepper, to taste

½ cup extra-virgin olive oil

2 cups store-bought tomato sauce

1 cup grated Parmigiano-Reggiano

1. Lay the egg roll wrappers in front of you with the corners at the top and bottom, like a diamond. Brush the surface lightly with water. Lay a piece of cheese on the lower third of the diamond. Season lightly with salt and pepper.

2. Roll the cheese in the wrapper halfway, then fold in the corners of the wrapper like a burrito. Continue rolling, and press to seal the edges.

3. Place a nonstick pan over medium-high heat and add about ⅛ inch of oil to the pan, or just enough to coat. Once the oil shimmers, place several mozzarella sticks in the pan. Let cook 1–2 minutes per side, or until golden brown all around.

4. Remove from oil to a paper towel-lined plate and season immediately with salt. Allow to cool slightly before serving.

5. Serve with marinara sauce for dipping and top with grated Parmigiano-Reggiano.

Grilled Lemon Oregano Chicken Wings

Serves: 8 / **Prep Time:** 24 hours / **Inactive Time:** 6 hours / **Cook Time:** 30 minutes

Courtesy of Michael Symon / From time to time, I like to take some of my favorite classic American dishes, like chicken wings or burgers, and go global. So here I've got a great chicken wing dish that will make my Greek relatives proud. It's a very simple and incredibly satisfying dish the whole family will love. I'm always amazed at the amount of flavor that you get out of just a few ingredients, which is a great lesson in the less-is-more approach to cooking. This dish is great for a tailgate gathering or just a leisurely summer meal out by the grill. Serve this with potato salad or grilled veggies in the summer or just lots and lots of napkins for the big game.

3 pounds chicken wings, split at the joint

½ cup plus 3 tablespoons extra-virgin olive oil

Zest of 2 lemons (save lemon halves for later)

2 garlic cloves, crushed

3 tablespoons honey

1 tablespoon kosher salt

Kosher salt and freshly ground black pepper, to taste

2 tablespoons fresh oregano leaves

1. Place the chicken and next five ingredients into a gallon-sized zip-top bag and place that on a plate or in a baking dish. Refrigerate for at least 6 hours.

2. Preheat the oven to 400°F. Preheat the grill to medium-high heat.

3. Spread the wings out on a baking tray with any liquid remaining from the marinade. Bake for 25–30 minutes, until just about cooked through.

4. Remove from the oven and let cool slightly. Then pat dry.

5. Drizzle the wings with 3 tablespoons of olive oil. Season with salt and freshly ground black pepper and add the picked oregano. Toss to evenly coat all of the wings.

6. Place the wings on the grill for 2–3 minutes per side, until they are nicely charred and warmed through. At the same time as the chicken wings, place the lemon halves on the grill cut side down.

7. Remove the wings to a platter and serve with the grilled lemon halves, squeezing the juice over the top.

Spaghetti Aglio e Olio

Serves: 6 / **Prep Time:** 10 minutes / **Cook Time:** 12 minutes

Courtesy of Mario Batali / This dish is one of the simplest, spiciest, and most delicious of the Italian pasta staples. Italians pride themselves on the quality of ingredients. It's not about technique or being the fanciest of chefs; it's all about buying the absolute best ingredients and showcasing them in the best possible way. This dish is less than fifty cents per portion, but with its perfect flavor combination, you'll never imagine that it is anything but pure luxury, my friends.

Kosher salt, to taste

1 pound spaghetti

⅓ cup extra-virgin olive oil, plus more

3 garlic cloves, peeled and thinly sliced

¾ cup pickled cherry peppers, thinly sliced

1 tablespoon red chili flakes

½ cup flat-leaf parsley

½ cup toasted bread crumbs

1. Bring a large pot of water to a boil over high heat and season generously with salt.

2. Cook the pasta for 1 minute less than the package instructions indicate.

3. Meanwhile, in a large sauté pan over medium-low heat, add about ⅓ cup of olive oil. Add the garlic, pickled peppers, and chili flakes. Add a tablespoon of pasta water to ensure the garlic doesn't brown. Cook gently until the garlic softens, about 8 minutes.

4. Remove the pasta from the water and transfer to the pan. Toss to coat and add a ladle full of reserved pasta water.

5. Drizzle with a healthy amount of olive oil and toss in the chopped parsley.

6. Serve in bowls and top with toasted bread crumbs.

Mushroom Fettuccine Alfredo

Serves: 4 / **Prep Time:** 2 minutes / **Cook Time:** 8 minutes

Courtesy of Clinton Kelly / I know that mushrooms and rosemary are not traditional ingredients in a classic Italian Alfredo, but I'm not a traditional kind of guy. I stumbled upon the idea for this one night when I was cleaning out my fridge and I had nothing in it but some fresh herbs and some mushrooms. I always have pasta on hand for when I don't feel like making anything fussy, and there is always butter and cheese in the Kelly household. Alfredo is basically just pasta tossed with cheese and butter, a blank canvas for whatever you have sitting in that fridge of yours. So if you're not an Italian purist, play around with whatever you've got. I know it will be delicious.

8 tablespoons unsalted butter, room temperature

2 tablespoons extra-virgin olive oil

1 pound cremini mushrooms, sliced

1 teaspoon chopped rosemary leaves

Kosher salt and freshly ground black pepper, to taste

1 pound fresh fettuccine

½ cup freshly grated Parmigiano-Reggiano

1. Bring a large pot of salted water to a boil.

2. Heat a large sauté pan over medium heat. Melt 2 tablespoons of butter in the pan and add a drizzle of olive oil. Add the mushrooms in an even layer, being careful not to crowd the pan. Allow the mushrooms to brown, stirring occasionally until cooked through. Sprinkle in the chopped rosemary, season with salt and pepper, and cook a minute more. Remove from heat and set aside.

3. Add the fresh pasta to the boiling water and cook for 2-3 minutes, or until al dente. Meanwhile, place the remaining butter into a large mixing bowl. Remove the pasta from the pot directly into the mixing bowl along with ¼ cup of pasta water. Quickly toss the pasta in the bowl and add in the cheese. Add another ¾ cup of pasta water to loosen and form a sauce, and stir in the browned mushrooms. Season with salt and pepper.

4. Serve with more freshly grated Parmigiano-Reggiano.

Chicken-Fried Chicken

Serves: 5 / **Prep Time:** 20 minutes / **Cook Time:** 20 minutes

Courtesy of Carla Hall / You know I'm a southern girl at heart, and when I find myself hungrier than a termite in a steel building, well there's no dish that satisfies my hunger like southern-style chicken-fried chicken: tender chicken cutlets, pan-fried and served with a creamy, velvety pan gravy. Nothing says simple, southern comfort like this.

FOR THE CHICKEN:

Kosher salt and freshly ground black pepper, to taste

5 boneless, skinless chicken breasts, pounded to ¼-inch thickness

2 cups all-purpose flour

4 eggs, beaten

2 cups vegetable oil

FOR THE GRAVY:

3-4 tablespoons of frying oil from chicken

3-4 tablespoons of dredging flour

2 cups chicken stock

½ cup milk

2 sprigs thyme

1. Season the chicken with salt and pepper.

2. Season the flour with salt and pepper. Whisk to combine.

3. Dredge the pounded chicken breasts in the flour, shake off the excess, then dredge in the eggs. Dredge again in the flour and then set aside on a platter to rest for 10 minutes.

4. Preheat a large cast iron skillet and add oil. Place over medium-high heat.

5. Add the chicken in batches so as not to overcrowd the pan. Cook the chicken on both sides until golden brown and cooked through, about 3-4 minutes per side.

6. Remove the chicken to a paper towel-lined plate to drain excess oil. Season with salt and pepper immediately.

7. Once you've cooked all of the chicken, drain off almost all the oil, leaving 3-4 tablespoons in the pan. Return the pan to the stove over medium-high heat.

8. Use 3-4 tablespoons of flour from the dredging flour. Whisk into the oil and cook until the flour is light brown and has a sandy consistency.

9. Slowly whisk in the chicken stock and bring to a boil. Whisk constantly, reducing the heat to a simmer. Once the gravy begins to thicken, add the milk and thyme. Continue to whisk until the gravy is thick and coats the back of a spoon. Taste and adjust seasoning.

10. Remove thyme sprigs before serving.

11. Serve the gravy over the chicken-fried chicken.

Shrimp in Acqua Pazzo

Serves: 4 / **Prep Time:** 20 minutes / **Cook Time:** 25 minutes

Courtesy of Mario Batali / I love this dish so much that I have decided if I ever have to choose my last meal, this dish will be course seven of one hundred. It's just that delicious. The name of this hearty, yet delicate stew literally translates to "shrimp in crazy water," and it is a classic Italian delicacy. It's a little spicy from the pepper and a little sweet from the fennel and wine; when paired with the acidity of the tomatoes, it gives you the most balanced experience your palate can enjoy.

6 tablespoons extra-virgin olive oil

½ red onion, thinly sliced

1 garlic clove, peeled and smashed

1 hot pepper, thinly sliced

½ bulb fennel, thinly sliced; fronds reserved for garnish

6 cherry tomatoes, halved

½ cup white wine

½ cup water mixed with 1 teaspoon sea salt

16 jumbo shrimp, peeled, heads and tails on

½ bunch flat-leaf parsley, chopped to yield ⅛ of a cup

1. In a 6-quart soup pot, heat the oil over medium heat until it shimmers. Add the onion, garlic, hot pepper, and fennel and cook until soft and light golden brown, 8–10 minutes.

2. Add the tomatoes, wine, and water, and bring to a boil. Lower the heat and simmer 10 minutes. Add the shrimp and simmer until cooked through, about 5 minutes. Pour into a bowl and garnish with fennel fronds and parsley.

Pan-Roasted Steak with Red Wine Sauce

Serves: 2–4 / **Prep Time:** 10 minutes / **Cook Time:** 15 minutes

Courtesy of Michael Symon / This meaty masterpiece, classic in many French bistros, is such a great dinner for two. If you're looking to impress someone new in your life, this is the dish for you. What I love most about it is that everything comes together so quick. You sear or brown your steak in the pan and then set it aside to rest and make your pan sauce right there in all of that delicious meaty goodness. A little red wine goes a long way as far as flavor is concerned, and the butter that finishes the dish is what makes you go back for more. Man, those French really know what they're doing over there.

2 12-ounce sirloin steaks

Kosher salt and freshly ground black pepper, to taste

3 tablespoons extra-virgin olive oil

1 pound button mushrooms, sliced

2 shallots, peeled and thinly sliced

3 cloves garlic, skin-on

1 bunch oregano, leaves only, chopped

1 cup red wine

2 tablespoons red wine vinegar

3 tablespoons unsalted butter

1. Season the steaks with salt and pepper.

2. Heat the olive oil in a large sauté pan over medium-high heat. Cook the steak, searing each side thoroughly, allowing the meat to brown, about 4–5 minutes per side for medium rare. Remove the steak from the pan and set aside on a platter to rest.

3. Add the button mushrooms to the pan, cooking for a minute before adding the shallots and garlic. Cook until everything has softened and the mushrooms are browned.

4. Add the oregano, and then deglaze the pan with the red wine and a splash of red wine vinegar. Cook to reduce the sauce by half, about 4–5 minutes. Add butter to pan and then stir in to finish the sauce.

5. Spoon sauce over the steak to serve.

Chicken Under a Brick

Courtesy of Mario Batali / To be successful in executing this dish, you really only need two things: a chicken and a brick. The rest of the ingredients are just accessories. Now if you don't have a brick, borrow one from your neighbor's yard, and if you don't have the chicken, well, then a trip to the store should do the trick. The combination of these two items is transcendental. The skin becomes so crispy and the meat so tender that it rivals any fried chicken recipe. Just make sure to wrap that brick in foil before you set it on top of the chicken. You don't know what's been running around in your neighbor's yard.

FOR THE BRINE:

5 quarts water

1½ cups kosher salt

1½ cups brown sugar

1 handful peppercorns

8 bay leaves

FOR THE CHICKEN:

1–1½ pounds chicken, halved with the backbone and breastbone removed

3 tablespoons olive oil

1 tablespoon smoked paprika

Kosher salt and freshly ground black pepper, to taste

SPECIAL EQUIPMENT:

1 brick, wrapped in foil

1. Boil 1 quart of water. Add kosher salt, sugar, peppercorns, and bay leaves to boiling water. Once salt and sugar have dissolved, add mixture to 4 quarts of cold water. Stir to dilute and mix well. Drop the chicken pieces in the brine and let them sit overnight. Rinse, pat dry.

2. Preheat grill or grill pan over medium heat.

3. Drizzle the chicken with the olive oil and sprinkle with the smoked paprika and salt and pepper.

4. Grill the chicken under a foil-wrapped brick on both sides for 8–10 minutes per side, or until the internal temperature reads 160°F.

Beer-Can Turkey

Serves: 12 / **Prep Time:** 10 minutes / **Cook Time:** 2 hours, 30 minutes

Courtesy of Michael Symon / What happens when you combine tailgating and Thanksgiving into one magnificent dish? Beer-Can Turkey of course! What is so totally awesome about this meal is that you get a perfectly crispy skin around the entire bird, not just the breasts, and it cooks in half the time of the classic roasted turkey you're used to having on your Thanksgiving table. I prefer to cook this out on my grill with the lid down, but you could easily bake this in the oven at 350°F. Just make sure you put a baking dish underneath to catch all of the drippings, and don't forget to save them for gravy. One bite and you're ready for your end zone dance.

1 12–15-pound turkey, rinsed and patted dry, cavity cleaned

2 25-ounce cans of lager-style beer

1 cup water

FOR THE DRY RUB:

3 tablespoons dried oregano

3 tablespoons garlic powder

2 tablespoons smoked paprika

2 tablespoons coriander, toasted and ground

1 tablespoon freshly ground black pepper

2 teaspoons kosher salt

Juice of 1 lemon

1. Preheat gas grill to 350°F.

2. Using a can opener, remove the top from one of the beers. Pour one of the beers into the roasting pan, then set the other beer in the center.

3. Combine the oregano, garlic powder, smoked paprika, coriander, salt, and pepper in a small bowl. Place the turkey on a cutting board. Squeeze lemon juice all over the inside and outside of the turkey. Rub the spice mix all over the outside and inside of the bird. Put extra seasoning inside the opened beer can. Place the seasoned turkey on top of the beer can, with the legs down. Pour 1 cup of water into the bottom of the

roasting pan. Place on the grill, being very careful to stabilize the bird. Close the lid of the grill and cook for 1 hour. Open the grill and spoon pan sauce over the turkey. Close the grill and cook for 1 more hour. Baste the turkey with juices from the bottom of the pan. If the turkey begins to look a little dark, tent the top with foil. Let cook for another 30 minutes, or until the internal temperature of the leg reaches 165°F.

4. Remove from the grill and baste one more time before tenting with foil and resting for 30 minutes. After 30 minutes, slice and serve.

Creamed Corn in Foil

Serves: 4 / **Prep Time:** 20 minutes / **Cook Time:** 30 minutes

Courtesy of Michael Symon / This is one of my go-to side dishes to take to a barbecue or summertime potluck because it's easy to put together in advance, it travels really well, and once I get to the party or barbecue I don't have to work very hard. I just throw the little packets on the grill for a few minutes to warm them up and then it's party time. Your friends will be so impressed by how much flavor is packed into these little bundles, and you'll be happy when it comes time to clean up, because with this summertime treat, there's no dish required.

2 tablespoons extra-virgin olive oil

¼ pound thick cut bacon, small diced

1 medium onion, diced

1 clove garlic, peeled and minced

Kosher salt and freshly ground black pepper, to taste

3 cups raw corn kernels

Zest and juice of 1 lime

1 cup vegetable stock

4 tablespoons crème fraîche

1. Preheat your grill to medium-high heat.

2. Place a large sauté pan over medium-high heat. When the pan is hot, add a drizzle of olive oil followed by the bacon. Cook until the bacon begins to crisp, 5-7 minutes, then add the onion and garlic with some cracked black pepper. Cook until the onion and garlic softens, another 5-6 minutes. Mix with the raw corn. Add the lime juice and zest and season with a good pinch of salt and some more freshly ground black pepper.

3. Lay out 4 large pieces of aluminum foil. Spoon the corn mixture onto the foil. Spoon crème fraîche over the top of each pile of corn. Bring the sides of each piece of foil up and add the stock, then seal each packet tightly. Place the packets directly on your grill and put the lid down. Cook without opening or moving for 15 minutes.

4. After 15 minutes, open the grill and carefully open the top of the foil to stir the corn. Reseal packets and close the grill lid, cooking another 15 minutes. Remove from the grill, and allow to cool for at least 10 minutes before serving.

Bagel Stuffing

Serves: 8 / **Prep Time:** 15 minutes / **Cook Time:** 40 minutes

Courtesy of Carla Hall / You know how they always have day-old bagels at your local bakery on sale because they are slightly stale? Well, I have the perfect use for those discounted delights. My bagel stuffing puts those dried-out little spheres to good use and is such an interesting twist on the classic Thanksgiving stuffing. I know that once you make this one, it will become a staple on your holiday table, year after year.

4 everything bagels, sliced in half, then sliced into quarters

2 tablespoons unsalted butter, melted

1 large yellow onion, diced

2 stalks celery, diced

2 cloves garlic, peeled and minced

Kosher salt and freshly ground black pepper, to taste

1¾ cups low-sodium chicken stock

¼ cup heavy cream

3 large eggs, lightly beaten

¼ cup chopped dill

1. Preheat oven to 400°F.

2. Place the bagel pieces on a baking sheet and put in the oven for 8–10 minutes, or until lightly toasted. Lower the temperature to 350°F after the bagels are removed.

3. Meanwhile, in a large skillet over medium heat, melt 2 tablespoons butter, add the onion, celery, and garlic, then sauté for 5–6 minutes, until translucent. Season with salt and pepper. Add the chicken stock and set aside.

4. In a large bowl, add the cream and eggs, then whisk together. Add the toasted bagels and the melted butter, vegetable, and chicken stock mixture; toss to combine.

5. In a buttered 9 x 13-inch casserole dish, shingle the bagels and add the remaining stuffing mixture. Place in oven for 25–30 minutes, until golden brown and slightly puffed.

6. Remove from oven. Let cool for 5 minutes. Garnish with chopped dill.

Molasses-Glazed Ham with Honey Butter

Serves: 8–10 / **Prep Time:** 20 minutes / **Cook Time:** 1 hour

Courtesy of Mario Batali / I like to switch up my holiday menu from year to year by choosing a different theme. This year we're going country! Nothing says country Christmas like a glazed ham on your holiday table. And I'm here to tell you that a delicious ham can be super easy, too. Just get yourself the pre-smoked and boneless variety from the grocery store or butcher shop and dress it up with a delicious sweet and tangy glaze. I promise you, you'll impress your friends and family without even breaking a sweat. I love to set aside some of the leftovers to make little ham-and-egg sandwiches on leftover rolls or biscuits in the morning for breakfast. It just doesn't get any better.

1 7-9-pound smoked boneless ham

FOR THE MOLASSES GLAZE:

½ cup molasses

Zest and juice of 1 orange

Zest and juice of 1 lemon

1 tablespoon dark brown sugar

1 tablespoon orange liqueur

2 teaspoons, plus ½ cup Dijon mustard

FOR THE HONEY BUTTER:

2 sticks unsalted butter

¼ cup honey

Kosher salt, to taste

1. Preheat oven to 325°F.

2. Place ham on a rack in a roasting pan. Set aside.

FOR THE MOLASSES GLAZE:

3. In a medium saucepan, over medium heat, add the molasses, the zest and juice of the orange and lemon, brown sugar, orange liqueur, and 2 teapoons Dijon mustard. Whisk to combine, then let simmer for 5 minutes. Set aside to cool slightly.

4. Brush the remaining mustard over the ham. Then brush the glaze over the ham and place in the oven for about an hour, or until the ham is warmed through and the internal temperature is 140°F.

FOR THE HONEY BUTTER:

5. In a medium bowl, add the softened butter, honey, and salt. Mix well to combine.

6. Thinly slice the baked ham. Place the butter on top and serve.

Candied Sweet Potatoes with Pecans

Serves: 8 / **Prep Time:** 5 minutes / **Cook Time:** 1 hour, 15 minutes

Courtesy of Carla Hall / If you spend your holidays south of the Mason-Dixon Line, you know all about candied sweet potatoes. These gems are not just any sweet potatoes; they are sprinkled with brown sugar and pecans and then topped with marshmallows. That's right, I said it . . . MARSHMALLOWS! I know it sounds a little weird if you've never had this dish, but it is so good. It's of course a little bit sweet, but the pecans give it such a nutty flavor, and combined with all of the savory items on the Thanksgiving table, it's the perfect antidote to the salty carbo-loaded feast.

4 pounds sweet potatoes

Kosher salt

5 tablespoons butter

⅔ cup brown sugar

½ cup orange juice

1 teaspoon cinnamon

½ teaspoon ginger

¼ cup bourbon

2 cups mini-marshmallows

½ cup pecan pieces

1. Preheat the broiler to high.

2. Cover potatoes with water, and add enough salt to water so it tastes like the sea. Bring to a boil. Reduce heat and simmer for 25 minutes or until just tender. Drain and let potatoes cool.

3. When cooled, peel and cut potatoes into ¼-inch thick rounds. Layer potatoes in greased 9 x 13 baking dish.

4. In small saucepan, combine butter, brown sugar, orange juice, cinnamon, ginger, a pinch of salt, and bourbon. Bring mixture to a boil and cook for about 2 minutes. Pour over potatoes.

5. Bake uncovered at 350°F for 40 minutes, or until brown. Increase temperature to 500°F and top with mini-marshmallows and pecans. Cook for 5 minutes or until pecans and marshmallows are lightly browned.

Use It Up!

Hey there. Ever wonder if there's a better way to use up that last bit of jam, syrup, or condiment left at the bottom of the jar or can before tossing it into the recycling? When you're face-to-face with stems, peels, or leftover sauces, just step away from the garbage. Instead of flushing that hard-earned money down the disposal, we've got some foolproof tips for turning those seemingly worthless remnants into culinary masterpieces. Here are just a few of our favorites.

Mario: I like to take the last two to three tablespoons of tomato sauce that you have coating the jar and add about two tablespoons of balsamic and red wine vinegar, some chopped herbs (like chives or parsley), and some extra-virgin olive oil, salt, and pepper. Put the top back on and shake it like you mean it! This makes a delicious vinaigrette to drizzle over a simple arugula and shaved Parmesan salad or grilled veggies.

Carla: Don't throw out that pickle juice you've got left in the fridge; you know, the jar that's got just a bunch of dill and garlic still floating at the bottom of it. You know what I use it for? Brining my chicken before I fry it. That's right, just add your chicken pieces to the pickle juice and let it sit overnight. Then the next day dredge in some flour and spices and fry those bad boys up. It's an easy way to add a sweet and salty flavor to your chicken inside and out.

Clinton: Real maple syrup is expensive, so if you think I'm letting one single drop of it go to waste, you are wrong. When I'm at the very end of my supply and there's not quite enough for my weekend pancakes, I make a cocktail! You'll need just about a tablespoon of syrup. Mix that with lemon juice, about two ounces of bourbon, and a splash of soda, served on the rocks with an orange peel and a cherry, and you've got yourself a Maple Bourbon Spritz!

Michael: I definitely save all of my empty peanut butter jars for one use and only one: making peanut sauce! When I have only about two or three tablespoons of peanut butter stuck to the sides of the jar, I like to add a couple of those soy sauce packets that you get from the takeout place, about a quarter-cup of olive oil, some ginger and scallions if you've got them, and a couple of dashes of hot sauce. This makes a great marinade for pork tenderloin or a dipping sauce for grilled beef or chicken skewers.

Chapter 2

One-Pot Perfection

If there is one thing that everybody hates about cooking, it's the cleanup. If it weren't for those pesky dishes, we'd be in the kitchen cooking up a storm all day long, right? Well, fear not, my friends, *the Chew* crew is coming to the rescue with mouthwatering recipes using only one pot!

In my family, everybody loves a one-pot dish. When there's little cleanup afterward and an entrée with huge flavors perfect for any gathering, how could you possibly go wrong? One of my favorite things about one-pot cooking is that it gives you the opportunity to use some of those tougher cuts of meat, like brisket or turkey thighs, that tend to be a little less expensive than their quick-cooking counterparts. These tougher cuts of meat take a little bit longer to cook, but I find that they make the best leftovers and I often make more than I need so that I can stretch the dish throughout the week.

After all, one-pot dishes are not just about low- and slow-cooked stove-top braises. We've got crowd-pleasing casseroles, breakfast hash, pasta baked in foil, and slow cooker dishes galore. Each one of these meals promises easy assembly, and once you've popped that baking dish in the oven, put the lid on the stew, or plugged in that slow cooker, you've got nothing but time to do the things you love, like binge-watch *Designated Survivor*.

—MICHAEL SYMON

Sweet Potato and Chicken Sausage Hash

Serves: 6 / **Prep Time:** 10 minutes / **Cook Time:** 20 minutes

Courtesy of Clinton Kelly / This is the perfect weekend brunch dish during those early autumn months, when the air turns crisp and the leaves are just starting to change. It's one of my favorite times of the year. It's the time when I get to say good-bye to salads and grilled veggies and hello to sausage and potatoes. I find this dish to be the ultimate crowd-pleaser. It's rich and decadent but good for you, as well. I use sweet potatoes and chicken sausage so that I can have seconds without feeling bad about it.

2 tablespoons extra-virgin olive oil, divided

1 pound loose breakfast chicken sausage

2 medium sweet potatoes, diced

1 small yellow onion, diced

¼ cup water

1 red bell pepper, diced

1 jalapeño, diced

2 tablespoons fresh sage, chopped

4 large eggs

Hot sauce

1. Preheat oven to 400°F.

2. In a large cast iron skillet over medium-high heat, add 1 tablespoon olive oil and chicken sausage. Using the back of a wooden spoon, break the sausage into small chunks, then cook until golden brown, about 5–7 minutes. Remove from skillet onto a plate. In the same cast iron skillet, add another tablespoon olive oil, sweet potatoes, and onion; cook until slightly soft and golden brown, about 10–12 minutes. Add water, red pepper, jalapeño, sage, and browned sausage. Mix to combine. Make 4 indents in the potato mixture, crack 1 egg into each indent, cover with foil and place in oven for 7–10 minutes, or until eggs are set.

3. Serve with your favorite hot sauce.

Greek Omelet

Serves: 2 / **Prep Time:** 5 minutes / **Cook Time:** 5 minutes

Courtesy of Michael Symon / There is nothing better on a Saturday morning after a long night out with your friends than spending the morning in a Greek diner. If you ask me, Greek diners are the only diners. I love the two-sided menu with what seems like hundreds of options and endless omelet combinations to choose from. Not everyone feels the same way about braving the restaurant brunch scene on the weekends, especially in New York City, where I live. So if you want the Greek experience but you don't want to leave the house, try my version of the classic twenty-four-hour special, the always tasty omelet.

½ tablespoon extra-virgin olive oil, plus more to drizzle

2 cups baby spinach

1 clove garlic

4 large eggs

½ teaspoon fresh oregano leaves

½ tablespoon unsalted butter

½ cup Greek feta, crumbled

Kosher salt and freshly ground black pepper, to taste

1. In a medium sauté pan over medium-high heat, warm the olive oil. Once hot, add the spinach and garlic, cooking until the spinach has wilted. Remove to a strainer set over a bowl, and press some of the liquid out with the back of a spoon. Set spinach aside.

2. Crack the eggs into a bowl with the oregano, and whisk with a fork. Set aside.

3. Warm a nonstick pan over medium heat. Add the butter to the pan, and once it foams and subsides, add the egg mixture. Move the outer edges of the eggs inward and cook until just set. Sprinkle the feta on one half along with the spinach mixture, then fold the eggs over. Season with salt and pepper. Slide the omelet onto a plate, drizzle with olive oil, and enjoy.

Slow Cooker Asian Barbecue Chicken Sammies

Serves: 8–12 / **Prep Time:** 10 minutes / **Cook Time:** 5 hours

Courtesy of Clinton Kelly / If you're like me, you can often find yourself making the same old chicken dinners night after night. Sometimes you just need a little help from your pantry to switch things up a bit. My barbecue chicken sammies are great for a hungry bunch of kids or even better as sliders at your next party. The best part about this dish is that I just throw everything into the slow cooker in the morning and I've got dinner ready to go by 6:00 p.m. without a bunch of pans to clean, which leaves me some time to do whatever I want. You can't beat that!

1½ pounds boneless, skinless chicken breasts

1 package hamburger potato rolls, split

FOR THE ASIAN BARBECUE SAUCE:

1 cup tomato paste

1 cup rice wine vinegar

1 cup light brown sugar

½ cup soy sauce

1 cup hoisin sauce

1 orange, juice and zest

3 cloves garlic, chopped

1 teaspoon chili flakes

Kosher salt and freshly ground black pepper, to taste

FOR THE SLAW:

1 head Napa cabbage, core removed and thinly sliced

¼ cup sliced, pickled ginger

2 tablespoons rice wine vinegar

1 tablespoon sesame oil

2 tablespoons sesame seeds, lightly toasted

SPECIAL EQUIPMENT:

Slow cooker

1. In a slow cooker, add chicken, tomato paste, vinegar, brown sugar, soy sauce, hoisin sauce, orange juice and zest, garlic, chili flakes, and salt and pepper. Cover and cook on low for 5 hours.

2. Meanwhile, make the slaw. In a large bowl, combine the Napa cabbage, pickled ginger, vinegar, sesame oil, and sesame seeds.

3. Remove chicken to a cutting board. Using 2 forks, shred the chicken and return to the slow cooker. Stir to coat chicken in the sauce.

4. To assemble, top roll with some pulled chicken and slaw. Place remaining half of bun on top.

Pasta e Fagioli (Pasta and Bean Soup)

Serves: 6 / **Prep Time:** 5 minutes / **Cook Time:** 1 hour

Courtesy of Mario Batali / There is no cold-weather dish closer to my heart than this pasta and bean soup. Almost every region in Italy has its own version of this dish. It is the perfect example of how very few ingredients can come together in a symphony of hearty flavors to warm your bones on even the coldest days. It's a Batali-family staple that I am hoping you'll enjoy on your table as often as we do.

2 tablespoons pork fatback or bacon, cut into small cubes

6 tablespoons extra-virgin olive oil

¼ cup finely chopped Italian parsley, plus more for garnish

1 medium Spanish onion, finely chopped

2 tablespoons tomato paste

8 cups chicken stock

3 cups cooked borlotti beans or kidney beans, rinsed and drained if canned

2 cups dried pasta scraps from making fresh pasta (or broken dried fettuccine)

Kosher salt and freshly ground black pepper, to taste

Parmigiano-Reggiano, for garnish

1. In a Dutch oven, heat the pork fat and 2 tablespoons of the olive oil over high heat until almost smoking. Add the parsley and onion and cook, stirring, until the onion is brown and soft, 8–10 minutes. Stir in the tomato paste, reduce the heat to medium, and cook for 10 minutes. Add the chicken stock and beans and bring to a boil. Lower the heat and simmer for 30 minutes.

2. Add the pasta and simmer for 10 more minutes. Remove from the heat, season with salt and pepper, and allow to rest for 10 minutes.

3. Divide the soup among 6 serving bowls. Drizzle with the remaining olive oil and garnish with more parsley and grated Parmigiano-Reggiano.

Spring Slow Cooker Soup with Turkey Meatballs

Serves: 6 / **Prep Time:** 20 minutes / **Cook Time:** 3 hours

Courtesy of Carla Hall / As you already know, we love a good slow-cooked meal here at *The Chew*. Slow cookers are magical. You throw some ingredients in the pot, push a couple of buttons, and in four to six hours . . . boom, dinner is served. Now my trick to making this spring-inspired dish is to let the meatballs simmer low and slow with my veggies and broth, and at the end, I punch up the flavor by adding some fresh herbs and citrus to the mix. You get that nice fresh spring feel even though you're cooking something for hours and hours. Delicious!

FOR THE TURKEY MEATBALLS:

1 pound ground turkey

1 large egg, lightly beaten

¼ cup bread crumbs

2 tablespoons parsley, finely chopped

2 tablespoons tarragon, finely chopped

Kosher salt and freshly ground black pepper, to taste

FOR THE SOUP:

2 bunches radishes, stems removed and diced

2 bunches carrots, peeled and sliced into ¼-inch rounds

1 bunch collards, deveined and thinly sliced

2 quarts chicken stock, divided

¼ cup parsley leaves

¼ cup tarragon leaves

¼ cup chives roughly chopped

FOR THE TURKEY MEATBALLS:

1. In a large bowl, add the turkey, egg, bread crumbs, parsley, and tarragon. Mix to combine. Season with salt and black pepper. Form into ½-inch balls and place on a baking sheet lined with parchment.

FOR THE SOUP:

2. To the slow cooker, add radishes, carrots, collards, and 7 cups of chicken stock. Add meatballs and season with salt and pepper. Cover, turn on high, and cook for 2–2½ hours or until vegetables are tender and meatballs are cooked through.

3. Meanwhile, in the carafe of a blender, add remaining 1 cup of chicken stock, parsley, tarragon, and chives, and blend until smooth. Add the blended chicken stock to the slow cooker during the last 10 minutes of cooking.

4. To serve, ladle the soup into bowls.

Carrot Ginger Soup

Serves: 6 / **Prep Time:** 5 minutes / **Cook Time:** 20 minutes

Courtesy of Clinton Kelly / I created this dish for a busy mom of three who was looking for an easy meal to whip up for her boys after a long day of school and winter sports. It's always a struggle to get a hot and healthy meal on the table when you're in a hurry. But with this easy and incredibly healthy soup, I've got you and your family covered all winter long. Fill a thermos and take it with you on your next ski trip or winter hike. I promise the whole family will love it.

1 tablespoon extra-virgin olive oil

1 onion, roughly chopped

2 cloves garlic, smashed

1 2-inch piece of ginger, peeled, roughly chopped

6 carrots, peeled, roughly chopped

1 teaspoon cumin

Pinch red pepper flakes

1 teaspoon honey

1 15-ounce can coconut milk

2 cups chicken stock

Kosher salt and freshly ground black pepper, to taste

1 lime, cut into wedges

2 tablespoons cilantro, chopped

1. In a large saucepan over medium-high heat, add olive oil.

2. Add onion, sauté until translucent, about 5 minutes.

3. Add garlic, ginger, and carrots, then sauté 2 more minutes.

4. Add cumin, red pepper flakes, honey, coconut milk, and stock and bring to a simmer.

5. Transfer the mixture to the carafe of a blender on the lowest setting and gradually increase; blend until smooth. Season with salt and pepper.

6. Serve with lime wedges and cilantro.

Shrimp with Tomato and Feta

Serves: 4–6 / **Prep Time:** 5 minutes / **Cook Time:** 12 minutes

Courtesy of Michael Symon / Who says that you can't mix cheese and shellfish together? Not the Greeks, that's for sure. The result of this unexpected combination of rich shrimp with tangy feta is pure perfection. I put a little cinnamon and coriander in mine to add a nice warmth to the brothy tomatoes. Top that with the shrimp and cheese and, after just a few minutes under the broiler, you have a delicious appetizer or dinner for two.

2 tablespoons extra-virgin olive oil

2 garlic cloves, minced

1 medium shallot, minced

2 cinnamon sticks

½ teaspoon coriander

½ cup white wine

4 cups whole San Marzano tomatoes, slightly broken, with their juices

Kosher salt and freshly ground black pepper, to taste

1 pound medium shrimp, peeled and deveined

¾ cup feta cheese, crumbled

Baguette or other bread, to serve

1. Preheat broiler to medium-high heat. Place a cast iron pan over medium heat. When the pan is hot, add the olive oil along with the garlic and shallot. Season with a large pinch of salt and cook, stirring occasionally, until the vegetables soften and become aromatic, about 2 minutes.

2. Add the cinnamon and coriander and sweat for a few seconds, and then deglaze with white wine. Reduce the wine by half (this should only take a minute), then add the tomatoes. Season the mixture with salt and freshly ground black pepper and bring to a simmer.

3. Season the shrimp with salt and freshly ground black pepper. Add the shrimp all at once to the simmering liquid, gently stirring. Cook until pink and slightly firm to the touch. Remove the pan from the heat and sprinkle the feta over the top, then broil until slightly golden.

4. Serve with some crusty or grilled bread.

Spicy Coconut Mussels

Serves: 3–6 / Prep Time: 10 minutes / Cook Time: 15 minutes

Courtesy of Clinton Kelly / When I eat this dish, I think of my first trip to New Zealand, where I ate a ton of mussels and drank even more crisp sauvignon blanc. It was one of the best trips that I have ever been on, and the mussels there were as fresh and delicious as you can get. I was always a little intimidated to cook shellfish, but mussels are suprisingly easy and incredibly impressive, and you can have this entire meal on the table in less than twenty minutes. Make sure you have a lot of crusty bread standing by. You won't want to waste a single drop of the broth.

2 tablespoons canola oil

½ cup Yukon Gold potatoes, peeled and cut into ½-inch cubes

½ cup green beans, ends trimmed, cut into ½-inch pieces

½ cup red bell peppers, thinly sliced 1-inch pieces

2 cloves garlic, grated

2 teaspoons fresh ginger, peeled and grated

¼ teaspoon red pepper flakes

1 teaspoon curry powder

Kosher salt and freshly ground black pepper, to taste

1 13.5-ounce can unsweetened coconut milk

1 cup chicken stock or water

3 pounds mussels, scrubbed and beard removed

Zest and juice of 1 lemon

¼ cup bamboo shoots

¼ cup fresh basil, roughly chopped

¼ cup scallions, thinly sliced

1. Place a large, high-sided sauté pan over medium-high heat and add the oil, potatoes, green beans, peppers, garlic, ginger, red pepper flakes, and curry powder. Season with salt and pepper. Sauté until fragrant, about 3–4 minutes. Add the coconut milk and stock, bring to a simmer, and cook until the potatoes are tender but still have a bite, about 10 more minutes. Add the mussels, lemon zest, and juice, and bring to a simmer. Cover with a lid and cook over high heat until all the mussels open.

2. Remove from heat and discard any mussels that did not open. Season with salt and pepper. Add the bamboo shoots, basil, and scallions, stir to combine, and serve.

Curry Chicken Potpie

Serves: 4–6 / Prep Time: 15 minutes / Cook Time: 45 minutes

Courtesy of Carla Hall / One of my favorite things to do when I'm developing recipes is to take a dish that I love from my childhood, like chicken potpie, and give it a little bit of a twist to make it current and also to reflect the kind of cook that I am now. I love global flavors, and adding Indian ingredients to this dish really ups the taste and gives you something that is comforting but at the same time interesting and unique. This style of cooking is a great way to get your family to try something new by taking what they know and love and just tweaking the flavors ever so slightly. So try it out; you won't be disappointed. I promise.

FOR THE CURRY CHICKEN FILLING:

3 tablespoons extra-virgin olive oil

2 medium yellow onions, ½-inch dice

3 medium carrots, ½-inch half-moons

1 large russet potato, peeled, ½-inch dice

3 cloves garlic, minced

3 tablespoons fresh ginger, peeled and minced

2 tablespoons Madras curry powder

1 tablespoon ground coriander

⅓ cup all-purpose flour

5 cups low-sodium chicken broth

1 13.5-ounce can coconut milk

1 store-bought rotisserie chicken, shredded

2 cups frozen peas, thawed

Kosher salt and freshly ground black pepper, to taste

FOR THE PUFF PASTRY CRUST:

1 sheet puff pastry dough

2 tablespoons unsalted butter, melted

1 teaspoon mustard seed

1 teaspoon ground cumin

½ teaspoon ground coriander

1 teaspoon kosher salt

1. Preheat oven to 375°F.

FOR THE CURRY CHICKEN FILLING:

2. In a deep cast iron skillet, heat olive oil over medium heat, add onions, carrots, potato, garlic, and ginger. Sauté until softened, about 5-7 minutes. Add the curry powder, coriander, and flour to coat the vegetables. Gradually pour the chicken broth over the vegetable mixture and bring to a boil. Lower to a simmer. Stir in the coconut milk, chicken, and peas. Season with salt and pepper. Remove from heat and set aside to cool slightly.

FOR THE PUFF PASTRY CRUST:

3. Roll out the puff pastry dough on a floured work surface to fit the cast iron skillet. Place dough on top of the curry chicken filling, then crimp the edges. Brush the top with melted butter. Combine the mustard seed, cumin, and coriander in a small bowl, then sprinkle over the pastry. Place in oven and bake for 15-20 minutes or until puff pastry is golden brown.

Colorado Green Chili with Chicken

Serves: 8–10 / **Prep Time:** 20 minutes / **Cook Time:** 35 minutes

Courtesy of Mario Batali / I'm a firm believer that you can't host a game-day feast without a piping-hot pot of chili simmering on the stove. It's a tradition, here at *The Chew*, for Mr. Symon and me to duke it out every year at our ultimate chili cook-off. It's usually pretty close, but this pot of chili sealed the deal for me this past year and allowed me to walk away with the glorious golden chili trophy and the title of "*The Chew*'s Chili King." Not too bad for an Italian chef from Seattle. The key to a perfect pot of chili is to take the time to build great flavor. So fill the pot with your ingredients and let it stew all day long, because greatness like this takes time.

3 tablespoons extra-virgin olive oil

1-pound slab of bacon, cut in 1-inch cubes

8 chicken thighs, boneless, skinless, and cut into 4 pieces each

Kosher salt, to taste

3 tablespoons ground cumin

1 tablespoon ground coriander

1 tablespoon cayenne

3 red onions, sliced

3 cloves garlic, peeled and chopped

3 Fresno chilies, chopped

3 tablespoons tomato paste

4 ancho chilies, soaked in hot water

2 chipotles in adobo

4 serrano chilies, chopped, plus additional for garnish, sliced

1 28-ounce jar tomatillo salsa

2 cups cilantro, roughly chopped, plus more for garnish

1 bunch scallions, sliced, plus more for garnish

12 corn tortillas

¼ cup sour cream, for garnish

8–10 lime wedges, for garnish

2 cups Cotija cheese

1. In a large Dutch oven, add 3 tablespoons olive oil and place over medium heat. Add bacon and cook until golden brown, then remove to a paper towel and set aside. Season chicken with salt, cumin, coriander, and cayenne. Add chicken to the Dutch oven and cook until golden brown, about 3 minutes per side. Remove chicken to a plate.

2. Add onions, garlic, and Fresno chilies and cook for 3 minutes. Add tomato paste and cook for 1 minute. Remove ancho chilies from water, reserving the water, and add to a blender with the chipotles in adobo. Blend until smooth. Add the pureed chilies to the Dutch oven with the serranos. Place the chicken and bacon back into the pot and add the tomatillo salsa and reserve ancho chili liquid. Bring to a boil, then lower to a simmer and cook until the chicken is tender, about 15 minutes. Add the cilantro and scallions and stir to combine. Serve with tortillas, and garnish with sour cream, limes, cilantro, scallions, and sliced serranos.

Braised Turkey Thighs with Spicy Kale

Serves: 10 / **Prep Time:** 10 minutes / **Cook Time:** 1 hour

Courtesy of Michael Symon / If you think that turkey can only be eaten on Thanksgiving, you're sorely mistaken. I believe that turkey should be treated like chicken's older and meatier sibling. You can prepare it in much the same way as chicken. The only difference is that it takes a little longer to cook. So don't think that you have to break out the fine china and roast the whole bird to enjoy a good turkey dinner. I like to buy turkey cut into parts and braise it over low heat. In this recipe, I braise my turkey with kale and potatoes, but feel free to play around with different veggies. Try using sweet potatoes or squash, or root vegetables like rutabaga or turnips. I think you'll be amazed at how unlike Thanksgiving a turkey can taste!

Kosher salt and freshly ground black pepper, to taste

4 bone-in, skin-on turkey thighs

2 tablespoons olive oil

2 cups red onion, thinly sliced

2 cups carrots, peeled and diced

1 jalapeño, sliced into rings

4 garlic cloves, sliced

1½ cups dry white wine

1 12-ounce can crushed San Marzano tomatoes

1 pound russet potatoes, peeled and sliced

2 bay leaves

2 pounds kale, roughly chopped

½ cup toasted bread crumbs

Grated zest of 2 lemons

½ cup chopped fresh flat-leaf parsley

2 tablespoons extra-virgin olive oil

1. If you have the time, liberally salt the turkey the night before and refrigerate overnight.

2. Allow the turkey to come to room temperature for half an hour before cooking. Pat the turkey dry and season with salt and pepper.

3. Preheat the oven to 375°F.

4. In a large Dutch oven, heat the olive oil over medium heat. When the oil is hot, put the turkey skin-side down in the pot. Cook for 3–4 minutes, until the turkey is well browned. Flip the pieces and cook for 3–4 minutes to brown the other side. Remove the turkey from the pot and set aside on a plate.

5. Add the onion and a good pinch of salt to the pot and cook for 1 minute. Add the carrots, jalapeño, and garlic, and cook for 2 minutes. Pour in the wine and scrape up the tasty browned bits from the bottom of the pan using a wooden spoon. Cook for about 4 minutes, or until wine is reduced by half. Add the tomatoes, potatoes, and bay leaves and bring to a simmer.

6. Adjust for seasoning, adding salt if needed. Add the kale. Cover the pot and cook for 5 minutes. Remove the lid and stir. Put the turkey thighs on top of the kale, put the lid back on, and put in the oven for 40 minutes, until the turkey is cooked through.

7. Meanwhile, in a small bowl, combine the bread crumbs, lemon zest, parsley, and extra-virgin olive oil.

8. Remove the turkey from the oven and discard the bay leaves. Top the turkey with the bread-crumb mixture. Serve family-style right from the pot.

The Chew: Quick & Easy

Slow Cooker Spicy Eggplant Sauce

Serves: 2 / **Prep Time:** 5 minutes / **Cook Time:** 4 hours, 20 minutes

Courtesy of Carla Hall / Picture this: It's August and it's really hot outside. Your garden is filling up with all kinds of delicious veggies, especially eggplant, and you want to cook them up, but the idea of turning on your stove top or oven makes you sweat just thinking about it. Well, this dish is perfect for such a dilemma. I just take all of my eggplant and add it to the slow cooker and it does all of the work for me. Then I freeze this sauce in small containers (enough for two servings at a time), and when I'm hungry for a delicious summer pasta, I cook my noodles and add in the sauce. It's also delicious to serve over some grilled or toasted bread for a quick appetizer. Plus, super easy!

3 tablespoons extra-virgin olive oil

2 medium eggplants, cut into 2-inch pieces

Kosher salt and freshly ground black pepper, to taste

1 yellow onion, chopped

3 garlic gloves, smashed

3 tablespoons tomato paste

1–2 teaspoons chili flakes

2 28-ounce cans whole peeled plum tomatoes

2 sprigs oregano

½ cup basil leaves, loosely packed

¼ cup balsamic vinegar

SPECIAL EQUIPMENT:

Slow cooker

1. Put 3 tablespoons olive oil and the eggplants in the slow cooker.

2. Add the onion and the garlic, along with the tomato paste and the chili flakes.

3. Pour the tomatoes, oregano, basil, and balsamic vinegar into the slow cooker and season with salt and pepper. Cover and cook on low for 4 hours. Season with salt.

4. Serve sauce with your favorite noodles, or store in an airtight container in the fridge for up to a week.

Summer Scafata

Serves: 4 / **Prep Time:** 20 minutes / **Cook Time:** 30 minutes

Courtesy of Mario Batali / A scafata is a vegetable stew traditionally found in most Italian homes in Umbria (a central region of the country). Italians typically serve this dish with fava beans and artichokes in the springtime. But in the summer, it's all about whatever is growing in your garden. My recipe calls for fennel, zucchini, and tomatoes, but feel free to use anything that you've got. Don't be afraid that the flavors won't go together. As Michael Symon always says, "If it grows together, it goes together."

¼ cup extra-virgin olive oil

1 pound pancetta, diced small

½ Spanish onion, thinly sliced

1 teaspoon hot red chili flakes

1 large fennel bulb, core removed and diced

1 cup water

2 pounds zucchini, cut into ½-inch-thick half-moons

2 pounds fresh, ripe tomatoes, or 1 can San Marzano tomatoes, roughly chopped

Kosher salt and freshly ground black pepper, to taste

4 fresh mint leaves, for garnish

1. In a 10- to 12-inch sauté pan or Dutch oven, combine the olive oil and pancetta and cook over medium heat until the pancetta is soft and translucent, about 6 minutes. Add the onion, red pepper flakes, and fennel, and cook until the fennel is tender, about 8 minutes.

2. Add the water, zucchini, tomatoes, and pepper, and cook until the zucchini and tomatoes have broken down a bit, about 10 minutes. Season with salt.

3. Tear the mint leaves into pieces, sprinkle over the scafata, and serve. This dish is also good at room temperature.

Spaghetti and Clams Foil Pack

Serves: 4 / **Prep Time:** 10 minutes / **Cook Time:** 12 minutes

Courtesy of Clinton Kelly / I developed this recipe with the help of our amazing test kitchen at *The Chew*. It's brilliant on so many levels. First, it's portable, and you can cook it in your oven, on the grill, or even on the campfire. But here's the best part: there's no mess. Just wrap the whole dish–pasta, clams, and all–in aluminum foil and you're ready to go. No mess, no stress–all around, it's the perfect dish. When the clams open, dinner's ready. Who would have thought that you could have spaghetti and clams out by the open fire at the beach?

1 pound spaghetti

3 pounds littleneck clams, rinsed and picked through

4 scallions, thinly sliced

1 cup dry white wine

½ teaspoon red pepper flakes

2 Fresno or red jalapeño peppers, thinly sliced

1 lemon, sliced into rounds

4 tablespoons unsalted butter

½ cup chopped fresh parsley

Extra-virgin olive oil

Kosher salt and freshly ground black pepper, to taste

1. Preheat grill to medium-high heat.

2. Bring a large pot of salted water to a boil. Cook spaghetti for 2–3 minutes. Remove and set aside.

3. Lay out 4 large rectangles of heavy-duty foil on a flat surface. Curl up the sides to create a bowl. Place a fourth of the spaghetti into each packet. Divide the remaining ingredients between the four foil packets and drizzle with olive oil.

4. Bring the long ends of the foil together and fold over twice to seal. Fold in the remaining sides to seal the packet, leaving room for steam. Place foil packets on the grill and close the lid. Cook for 10 minutes, or until the clams have opened.

5. Remove from grill and serve immediately.

Arroz con Pollo

Serves: 6 / **Prep Time:** 5 minutes / **Cook Time:** 30 minutes

Courtesy of Mario Batali / To me, there is nothing more comforting than chicken and rice. It's one of the most basic but still most incredibly satisfying dishes. I think that's why almost every culture across the globe has its own version. In Spain, you've got paella; India has chicken biryani; in New Orleans, you've got jambalaya. This recipe is a Latin favorite, simply called arroz con pollo (or rice with chicken). Add spices and fresh herbs, and then bathe in wine and tomato before finishing with olives and a bright aioli to bring the whole thing together. This will give you a symphony of flavors anyone on earth would crave.

3 tablespoons extra-virgin olive oil

1 3½- to 4-pound chicken, cut into 8 pieces

Kosher salt and freshly ground black pepper, to taste

1 Spanish onion, roughly chopped

1 red bell pepper, roughly chopped

3 garlic cloves

1 teaspoon smoked paprika

2 tablespoons tomato paste

2½ cups long grain rice

½ cup dry white wine

2½ cups chicken stock

1–2 teaspoons saffron

1 bay leaf

¼ cup pitted and chopped green olives

3 tablespoons fresh chopped parsley, to garnish

2 tablespoons fresh chopped cilantro, to garnish

FOR THE JALAPEÑO AIOLI:

2 egg yolks

1 jalapeño, finely minced

1 clove garlic, finely minced

1 lime, juiced and zested

1 cup extra-virgin olive oil

1. Heat a Dutch oven over medium-high heat with a few tablespoons of olive oil. Season the chicken liberally with salt and pepper on all sides. Working in batches, brown the chicken on all sides. Remove from pan to a plate.

2. Combine the onion, pepper, and garlic in a food processor and pulse until finely chopped. Add to the pan with more oil as needed. Season with salt. Cook for 3-4 minutes until soft and slightly caramelized. Season with smoked paprika.

3. Add tomato paste and allow to cook until darkened. Once tomato paste is dark plum colored, add white rice and toast for 2 minutes.

4. Deglaze pan with white wine, then pour in chicken stock. Stir in the saffron, bay leaf, and olives and top with chicken. Bring to a boil, then reduce to a simmer. Cover and cook for 15–20 minutes, until rice is cooked.

5. Serve arroz con pollo warm with parsley, cilantro, and jalapeño aioli.

FOR THE JALAPEÑO AIOLI:

6. Whisk together the egg yolks, jalapeño, garlic, lime juice and zest, and a pinch of salt and freshly ground pepper. Whisk in the olive oil until emulsified.

Thankful Hoppin' John

Serves: 4–6 / **Prep Time:** 10 minutes / **Cook Time:** 25 minutes

Courtesy of Carla Hall / Hoppin' John, as all of you southerners know, is just a fancy title for peas and rice. This dish is a staple on my New Year's table because down south it's good luck to eat black-eyed peas as you celebrate the New Year. This dish symbolizes wealth and prosperity in the New Year, and if eating a delicious meal will bring me happiness all year long, I'm in. This dish also makes a great addition to any holiday table, but it goes especially well with pork.

2 tablespoons extra-virgin olive oil

1 large onion, diced

2 celery stalks, diced

2 cloves garlic, minced

1 tablespoon fennel seeds, toasted

1 tablespoon tomato paste

½ cup white wine

1 15-ounce can crushed tomatoes

1 cup water

1 cup long grain Carolina rice

Kosher salt and freshly ground black pepper, to taste

1 15-ounce can black-eyed peas, drained and rinsed

FOR THE GARNISH:

½ bunch scallions, sliced

½ bunch fresh cilantro, chopped

1 lime, cut in wedges

Hot sauce, to taste

1. In a 12-inch cast iron skillet over medium-high heat, add olive oil, onion, celery, garlic, and fennel seeds. Cook for 5 minutes or until translucent. Add the tomato paste, cook for 2 minutes. Add the wine, crushed tomatoes, and water. Let the mixture come to a simmer. Add the rice and cover. Cook for 20-25 minutes over low heat. Once the rice is tender, season with salt and pepper.

2. Stir in the black-eyed peas and let warm through. Remove from heat.

3. To serve, top with scallions, cilantro, lime juice, and hot sauce.

Braised Chicken with Potatoes and Tarragon

Serves: 6 / **Prep Time:** 5 minutes / **Cook Time:** 40 minutes

Courtesy of Mario Batali / We all know that meat and potatoes make a great weeknight meal, and I have this very easy recipe that always satisfies and always comes out perfectly tender and incredibly flavorful. I use bone-in chicken that I sear to a deep golden brown. After that step, you just throw everything into the pot, cover it for about thirty minutes, and then you've got dinner on the table without even breaking a sweat. And the best part: you've got only one pot to clean

1 3-pound chicken cut into 8 pieces

Kosher salt and freshly ground black pepper, to taste

2 tablespoons extra-virgin olive oil

1 red onion, sliced

6–8 cloves garlic, thinly sliced

1 pound new potatoes, quartered

2 tablespoons tomato paste

2 cups water (approximately)

¼ cup fresh tarragon leaves, roughly chopped

1. Preheat oven to 450°F.

2. Dry chicken well and season with salt and pepper.

3. Place a large cast iron pan or high-sided, ovenproof skillet over medium-high heat and add the oil. Add the chicken, skin-side down, and cook until well browned on both sides, about 10 minutes total. Remove chicken to a plate and set aside. Add the onion, garlic, potatoes, and tomato paste, and sauté for 3–4 minutes. Season with salt and pepper to taste. Add the browned chicken and the juices back into the pan, nestling the meat among the vegetables. Add enough water around the chicken so that the skin is still exposed. Bring to a boil. Remove from heat and place in the oven. Cook until the potatoes are tender and chicken is cooked through, about 30–40 minutes. Garnish with fresh tarragon and serve.

Kielbasa with Cabbage and Potatoes

Serves: 8–10 / **Prep Time:** 20 minutes / **Cook Time:** 35 minutes

Courtesy of Michael Symon / Nothing reminds me of my hometown of Cleveland, and my childhood, like the flavors of kielbasa and cabbage. There is this great place in Cleveland called the West Side Market. It's this huge building with meat as far as the eye can see, and it is the home of the best kielbasa anywhere. This dish is so incredibly easy to make and the flavors are so rich and surprising considering how few ingredients there are. It has everything you could want on a cool winter day—and you could even throw everything into your slow cooker if you want and have the best-smelling house on the block.

2 tablespoons olive oil

1 whole kielbasa

1 yellow onion, sliced

½ head green cabbage, sliced

½ pound new potatoes, halved

Kosher salt and freshly ground black pepper, to taste

12 ounces lager-style beer

3 tablespoons spicy brown mustard

Baguette or other bread, to serve

1. In a large Dutch oven, heat the olive oil over medium-high heat. Add kielbasa and sear until brown, 3 minutes per side. Remove from pan. Add onion and cabbage and cook for 3-4 minutes. Add potatoes and kielbasa, and season with salt and pepper. Fill pot three-fourths the way up with beer and simmer, uncovered, until potatoes are tender, about 20 minutes.

2. Remove from heat and stir in mustard. Serve with crusty bread.

Slow Cooker Braised Short Ribs

Serves: 8 / **Prep Time:** 10 minutes / **Cook Time:** 4–6 hours

Courtesy of Michael Symon / If you ask me, easy doesn't always have to be quick. Now there is a time and a place for fast recipes, but sometimes delicious food is worth waiting for, like my braised short ribs. It used to be that short ribs were a luxury item, but now you can find them in any supermarket across the country. This cut of meat needs to be cooked over low heat for a few hours. I like to get everything in the pot in the morning and let it do its thing while I catch up on my shows or veg out on the couch watching a good movie. Talk about a relaxing weekend!

6-8 bone-in short ribs

Kosher salt and freshly ground black pepper, to taste

2 tablespoons extra-virgin olive oil

1 medium onion, peeled and diced

1 jalapeño, sliced into thick rings

3 cloves of garlic, peeled and smashed

1 1-inch piece of fresh ginger, sliced

1½ quarts water

1 cinnamon stick

2 whole star anise

1 teaspoon whole coriander

SPECIAL EQUIPMENT:

Slow Cooker

1. Preheat your slow cooker to high. Season your short ribs on each side with salt and pepper. When the slow cooker is hot, add a film of oil followed by the seasoned short ribs. Sear for 3-4 minutes per side until they are deep golden brown. Don't overcrowd the pot. Sear in batches to avoid steaming. As the short ribs are seared, remove them to a plate and set aside.

2. When all of the short ribs have been seared, add the onion, jalapeño, garlic, and ginger with a pinch of salt. Next add the water and bring to a simmer. Taste the cooking liquid at this point, adding additional salt and pepper if necessary. Add the cinnamon stick, star anise, and coriander. Add the short ribs back in, cover with a lid, and cook on high for 4-6 hours, until meat is very tender and falling off the bone. Serve with mashed potatoes or buttered egg noodles if you'd like.

One-Pot Holiday Pork Roast

Serves: 8–10 / Prep Time: 15 minutes / Cook Time: 1 hour, 15 minutes

Courtesy of Carla Hall / When was the last time you cooked an entire holiday meal in one pot? I know it definitely wasn't Thanksgiving! Here I am offering just that. A holiday party in a pot. It's got all of those classic flavors—apples and cinnamon, rosemary and apple cider— that you love to eat around Christmas and New Year's, and it's super impressive when you present it to your friends and family at your table. And they'll never know that you got all those ingredients into that one single pot in less than ten minutes.

4 pounds center-cut pork loin, boneless

Kosher salt and freshly ground black pepper, to taste

2 tablespoons extra-virgin olive oil

1 tablespoon rosemary, chopped, plus more full sprigs for garnish

2 sweet potatoes, cut into 1½-inch wedges

2 red onions, cut into 1½-inch slices

1 Granny Smith apple, cored, cut into 1½-inch wedges

1 orange, cut into 8 wedges

3 parsnips, peeled, cut into 3-inch pieces

2 cinnamon sticks

3 whole star anise

1 cup apple cider

1. Preheat oven to 375°F.

2. Season pork loin all over with salt and pepper. Drizzle with olive oil and rub rosemary all over the pork.

3. In a large high-sided cast iron pan or Dutch oven, add the sweet potatoes, red onions, apples, oranges, parsnips, cinnamon sticks, star anise, and a few sprigs of rosemary. Spread the ingredients into an even layer to make a bed for the pork. Lay the pork on top of the bed of fruit and vegetables. Pour the apple cider into the bottom of the pan.

4. Place in the oven to roast until the internal temperature reaches 145°F, about 1 hour and 15 minutes.

5. Remove roast to a cutting board and tent with aluminum foil. Let rest for 20 minutes before slicing. Serve with roasted vegetables.

A Pan and a Plan

We are all in agreement here at *The Chew*, a sheet-pan meal is where it's at. Dirtying one sheet pan is not the worst thing in the world when you think about how many dishes you've been known to mess up in search of a good meal. We have figured out a way to make cleanup even easier: foil! We cover our sheet pans with aluminum foil before we put them in the oven; when dinner's ready, just take the foil off, throw it in the recycling, and boom, you've got yourself a mess-free meal the whole family will love. Here are just a few of our favorite versions of the classic sheet-pan fare.

Clinton Kelly: My go-to sheet-pan meal is actually a delicious and nutritious breakfast. For my favorite granola recipe, I take about three cups of rolled oats and then half a cup of everything else: raisins, cranberries, sesame seeds, almonds, vegetable oil, and honey. Mix that all together and set it on a baking sheet and let it toast in the oven for about forty-five minutes at 350°F. Just give it a stir a couple of times throughout the cooking and you've got a delicious breakfast that will last for weeks in your pantry.

Mario Batali: My favorite sheet-pan dinner is the obvious choice: pizza. Crank your oven up to 450°F, and while it's preheating roll out some pizza dough, drizzle with olive oil, and then add some thinly sliced new potatoes, some red onion, and rosemary. Season with a little salt and pepper, and into the oven it goes—no foil required. This dish takes about ten to fifteen minutes before it's on the table ready to go.

Michael Symon: I would argue that salmon is the greatest sheet-pan dinner possible. I take a big piece of skin-on salmon and cook it really low at 250°F to keep it moist and tender. Lay some whole scallions beside it, drizzle with some honey and soy sauce, season with a little salt and pepper, and pop it in the oven. For a one-pound piece of salmon, I'd keep it in the oven for about twenty minutes.

Carla Hall: You know I can't resist going to the sweeter side of this challenge. A sheet-pan dessert can be just as easy as a savory dinner option. My number one sheet-pan dessert involves figs. I take about ten figs, halve them, sprinkle with a little sugar, and pop in the oven for about ten to fifteen minutes. The sugar helps all of those delicious juices ooze out of the tender figs to create a rich syrup. Top the figs with a little vanilla ice cream, some toasted pistachios, and a little of that sweet syrup. It's so light and easy. I'd even throw biscotti in there for fun if you're feeling crazy!

Chapter 3

Effortless Entertaining

We know from your countless letters and tweets that entertaining anytime of the year (but especially around the holidays) stresses you out more than just about anything else in the world. We've taken in all of your notes, and we want you to know that we are here for you. Entertaining should be fun; it should be about friends and family, and spending time with the people you love. It should definitely not be about proving to everyone you know that you are just as talented at hosting a party as Martha Stewart. If you go in with that attitude, you're just setting yourself up for failure.

We think throwing a dinner party should be painless, so don't make yourself crazy. Just pick a few dishes that you've made before and that you know will be successful. If you're going to experiment, pick one or two new dishes to try. We have thought long and hard about the best advice for easy and effortless entertaining and have come up with some really interesting ideas that will impress your friends and family without sending you to the psych ward. We've got appetizers you can put together in under a minute, make-ahead meals, plating tips, and timeless holiday dishes you'll be proud to call your own.

—*THE CHEW HOSTS*

Summer Sangria

Serves: 8 / **Prep Time:** 5 minutes / **Inactive Time:** 4–24 hours

Courtesy of Clinton Kelly / It's always five o'clock somewhere, which means right now is the perfect time to have a drink. If I'm having a party outdoors in the summertime, this sangria is always my go-to cocktail. The reason I love this drink so much is that you can make it the night before right in the pitcher and let the flavors come together in the fridge, and the next day it's ready to go when your guests arrive. No mixing or shaking required, which means you get to enjoy your party instead of playing bartender for hours on end.

3 oranges, cut into rings

2 lemons, cut into rings

3 peaches, pitted and diced

3 bottles pinot grigio

8 ounces brandy

8 ounces orange-flavored liqueur

1 pint strawberries, hulled and halved

Place oranges, lemons, and peaches in a large pitcher or punch bowl. Add wine, brandy, and liqueur. Refrigerate 4–24 hours to allow the fruit to infuse. When ready to serve, ladle into glasses over ice and serve garnished with strawberries.

Ham and Cheese Puff Pastry Pinwheels

Serves: 10 / **Prep Time:** 15 minutes / **Cook Time:** 15 minutes

Courtesy of Carla Hall / When you throw your next dinner party I want you to be successful. I want you to shine, and a little store-bought help can often be the key to effortless entertaining. Why make life hard when you can make delicious food without stress? It's a no-brainer. That's why these little ham and cheese pinwheels are so easy to make, and once you get the method down, feel free to play with the flavors a bit. Bacon and caramelized onions, spinach and mushrooms, you can even make these little guys into dessert by rolling up some cinnamon and sugar inside. The possibilities are endless!

1 8-ounce block cream cheese, softened

2 tablespoons butter, softened

3 sprigs thyme, leaves only

½ cup Gruyère, shredded

¼ teaspoon ground cloves

Kosher salt and freshly ground black pepper, to taste

1 sheet puff pastry, thawed

¼ pound thinly sliced ham

½ cup pitted green olives, chopped, for garnish

Zest of half an orange, for garnish

2 tablespoons honey, for garnish

1. Preheat oven to 400°F. Line baking sheet with parchment paper.

2. In a medium bowl, add the cream cheese, butter, thyme, Gruyère, and cloves, season with kosher salt and freshly ground black pepper, and mix to combine.

3. Place the thawed puff pastry on a floured surface. Spread the cream cheese mixture evenly over the puff pastry. Add the ham evenly over the top.

4. Beginning with the short side of the pastry, roll to seal. Cut into 10 slices and place cut-side down on the baking sheet. Bake for 15–20 minutes or until golden and crispy. Remove from the oven and allow to cool on a wire baking rack for 10 minutes. Garnish with chopped olives, orange zest, and a drizzle of honey.

Prosciutto with Baked, Stuffed Figs

Serves: 4 / **Prep Time:** 5 minutes / **Cook Time:** 10 minutes

Courtesy of Mario Batali / October is when figs are at their finest. I like to pair them with what I call the undisputed queen of cheeses: Gorgonzola dolce. It's a milder blue cheese that doesn't overpower the delicate flavor of the figs. Roast those in the oven just to melt the cheese and soften the figs and place them over some strategically arranged pieces of prosciutto, and you've got yourself a five-star appetizer for even the toughest critic.

12 figs, stems trimmed

6 ounces Gorgonzola cheese, room temperature

2 tablespoons walnuts, finely chopped, plus ½ cup roughly chopped

½ cup parsley, chopped

4 ounces prosciutto, thinly sliced

1. Preheat oven to 450°F.

2. In the top of each fig, cut an X shape, leaving them intact at the base. Place on an ungreased baking sheet and gently open.

3. In a small bowl, add the Gorgonzola, walnuts, and parsley and mix to combine. Using a spoon, stuff each fig with 1 tablespoon filling. Bake figs for 8-10 minutes, until the cheese filling begins to bubble.

4. On serving plates, arrange 3 or 4 slices of prosciutto. Place 3 figs in the center of each plate, sprinkle with remaining walnuts, and serve warm.

Feta and Dill Tiropita

Serves: 16 / **Prep Time:** 10 minutes / **Cook Time:** 25 minutes

Courtesy of Michael Symon / These little packets of goodness were a staple at my house growing up around the holidays, but especially around Easter (when the weather warms up a bit and you're craving something a little lighter than those soups and stews of winter). I love these bundles because you can fill them with anything and they freeze really well. I have a whole tray of these in my freezer right now just waiting to bake when I have my next party.

2 cups crumbled feta

1 cup plain Greek yogurt, strained

1 large egg, scrambled

2 tablespoons finely chopped fresh dill

½ teaspoon kosher salt

1 teaspoon freshly ground black pepper

3 pieces phyllo dough, thawed

1 stick unsalted butter, melted

1. Preheat oven to 350°F.

2. In a mixing bowl, combine the feta, yogurt, egg, dill, salt, and pepper. Mix to thoroughly combine, then set aside.

3. Lay out the sheets of phyllo vertically, with the short end closest to you. Cut in half lengthwise. Brush with melted butter and fold the piece of dough in half lengthwise. Place 1 tablespoon of the filling in the bottom right corner of the sheet of dough. Begin to fold upward in the shape of a triangle. Continue to fold up the sheet until you reach the top. Brush with butter and place on a baking sheet. Repeat with the remaining pieces of phyllo and filling.

4. Place the triangles on a parchment-lined sheet tray and continue to form the tiropita. Brush the tops with melted butter and bake for 25 minutes, until light golden brown and puffed.

Salami Cornucopia

Courtesy of Clinton Kelly / This is an appetizer that is as fun to eat as it is to put together. I came up with this dish when Carla challenged me to make a delicious appetizer, perfect for a party, in sixty seconds or less. That's right, in a minute, tops. Well, I pulled it off with a few seconds to spare. Talk about effortless entertaining! I creamed together some soft cheeses, stirred in some olives, herbs, and spices, and rolled them up into the cutest little cones. Just genius if I do say so myself.

1 8-ounce block of cream cheese, softened

1 8-ounce log goat cheese, softened

½ cup black olives, chopped

1 teaspoon crushed red pepper

1 teaspoon fresh thyme leaves

1 lemon, zested

25 slices salami, thinly sliced

1. In a large bowl, add the cream cheese, goat cheese, olives, crushed red pepper, thyme, and lemon zest, and mix to combine. Place mixture in a piping bag and cut the tip with scissors.

2. Fold each piece of salami into a cone shape. Pipe the filling into the center of the cornucopia until filled, and place seam-side down on a platter. Repeat until all are filled. Serve with crudités if you'd like.

Baked Beef Sliders

Serves: 6 / **Prep Time:** 5 minutes / **Cook Time:** 7–10 minutes

Courtesy of Carla Hall / My perfect guilty pleasure food is a burger. A burger stacked high, but not too high, with toppings on a brioche bun is pure heaven for me. As a former caterer, I am always on the lookout to find classic dishes that everyone loves and turn them into something small that you can serve as an appetizer at a party. I wanted to figure out a way to serve sliders to a crowd without having to stand at the stove like a short-order cook all day long, because I want to party, too. I finally figured it out. You just bake them! In less than ten minutes you've got burgers for a crowd. How awesome is that?

1 pound lean ground beef

Kosher salt and freshly ground black pepper, to taste

½ pound sliced yellow cheddar cheese

½ cup mayonnaise

½ cup Dijon mustard

6 slider buns

SPECIAL EQUIPMENT:

1 6-cup cupcake tray

1. Place a 6-cup cupcake tray in the oven and preheat to 450°F.

2. Meanwhile, divide the meat into 6 round patties in the same size as the cupcake circles in the tray. Season both sides of the patties with salt and pepper. When the oven is preheated, carefully and quickly place the formed patties into the cupcake tray using tongs. Bake for 5 minutes. Remove and top with the cheese and place back in the oven, just until the cheese is melted.

3. In a separate bowl, mix together the mayonnaise and the Dijon mustard. Set aside.

4. Smear some Dijonnaise on the slider buns. Serve cooked sliders on slider buns and enjoy.

The Chew: Quick & Easy

Chicken and Shrimp Dumplings

Serves: 12 / **Prep Time:** 45 minutes / **Cook Time:** 15 minutes

Courtesy of Clinton Kelly / I think that there is so much potential in a dumpling, not only within the flavor profiles but in the way that you present them. I love to serve these little guys when I have a cocktail party because they are so chic-looking. I just grab a bunch of those Asian-style soup spoons that you can find at any home-goods store and put about one to two tablespoons of the dipping sauce in the bottom of the spoons. When I finish steaming my dumplings, I add one to each of the spoons and then either set them out on my buffet table or walk them around as passed appetizers. In my opinion, It's the details that really elevate a cocktail party.

FOR THE DUMPLINGS:

2 cups chicken stock

½ pound ground chicken

½ pound shrimp, peeled and deveined

2 garlic cloves, chopped

2 teaspoons fresh ginger, grated

3 scallions, chopped

1 tablespoon soy sauce

2 teaspoons toasted sesame oil

1 small bunch cilantro stems only

1 egg

25 round wonton wrappers

FOR THE SPICY GINGER DIPPING SAUCE:

½ cup soy sauce

2 tablespoons ginger, minced

3 tablespoons hot sauce

2 tablespoons lime juice

FOR THE DUMPLINGS:

1. Bring 1 quart of water and 2 cups of chicken stock to a boil in a medium stockpot fitted with a strainer basket. Reduce to a simmer.

2. In the bowl of a food processor, add the chicken, shrimp, garlic, ginger, scallions, soy sauce, sesame oil, cilantro, and egg, and pulse until fully combined.

3. Brush a wonton wrapper with water. Place 2 teaspoons of the chicken and shrimp mixture into the center of the wrapper. Pinch sides of the wrapper together to form four points. Press the creases in a clockwise fashion to the side of the wonton pouch (the top of the dumpling should be open). Repeat with the remaining wrappers and filling.

4. Place the dumplings into a steamer basket that has been lightly sprayed with nonstick spray, making sure the edges do not touch, working in batches.

5. Place the steamer basket into the stockpot and cover with a lid. Cook for 12-15 minutes. Gently remove the dumplings to a serving platter along with the dipping sauce.

FOR THE SPICY GINGER DIPPING SAUCE:

6. In a medium bowl, add the soy sauce, ginger, hot sauce, and lime juice, and mix to combine. Serve with the dumplings.

Alsatian Tarte Flambé

Serves: 6–8 / **Prep Time:** 15 minutes / **Cook Time:** 20 minutes

Courtesy of Mario Batali / At my house, we make tarte flambé for our movie nights, when the whole family stays in to cozy up to a good comedy or suspense thriller. What is tarte flambé you ask? Well, it's basically the French version of pizza. It's bacon-y, and cheesy, and potato-y, and it's the perfect indulgence. Originally, this dish was the French baker's test to make sure that the oven was the perfect temperature. The baker would take some bread dough and whatever ingredients were available and pile them up and toss them into the oven. If the oven was too hot, you had a fiery mess, hence the term flambé. But if the oven was just right, you had a delicious dish, perfect for any meal: breakfast, lunch, or dinner.

1 pound store-bought
pizza dough

FOR THE TOPPING:

Kosher salt and freshly ground
black pepper, to taste

2 russet potatoes, peeled

½-pound slab bacon,
cut into cubes

1 tablespoon of extra-virgin
olive oil

1 large Spanish onion, sliced
thinly

3 cloves garlic, minced

2 ounces kirsch or grappa

½ cup crème fraîche

⅓ cup Emmentaler or Gruyère
cheese

⅓ cup ricotta

¼ cup chives, chopped

1. Preheat the oven to 400°F.

2. Take the pizza dough out of the fridge and let sit for about 20 minutes.

FOR THE TOPPING:

3. Bring a pot of water to a boil and season generously with salt. Cook the potatoes until they can be pierced easily with a knife. Remove from the water and let cool. Slice the potatoes into ⅛-inch round slices.

4. Place the bacon in a large cast iron skillet. Add a tablespoon of olive oil so the bacon doesn't stick. Cook over medium-low heat until crisp and brown. Remove the bacon from the pan and reserve on paper towels.

5. Add the onion to the pan, season with salt. Add the minced garlic and pull the pan off the

heat. Carefully pour in the kirsch or grappa.

6. Combine the crème fraîche, cheese, and ricotta. Add about 20 turns of cracked black pepper and ½ teaspoon of salt.

7. Roll the dough out into a 10-inch circumference. Lay the dough on a greased sheet tray. Place in the preheated oven and bake for about 4 minutes. Remove the dough from the oven. Smear the dough with the cheese mixture, and shingle the potatoes in a pinwheel pattern. Place an even layer of the caramelized onions on the potatoes and sprinkle the bacon on top of the onions. Top with a bit more grated cheese.

8. Return the dough to the oven until it is crisp on the bottom and the toppings are bubbly, 6–8 minutes. Sprinkle with chives and serve.

Quesadilla Party

Serves: 8–12 / **Prep Time:** 10 minutes / **Cook Time:** 10 minutes

Courtesy of Carla Hall / Ain't no party like a quesadilla party! Am I right? Well, if you've never thrown one of these little shindigs, you are missing out. It's so fun and festive—and so easy to put together for your next barbecue or outdoor birthday party. I like to fill a bunch of flour tortillas with cheese for my guests and set them out on a platter. Then I grill some chicken and beef and some veggies and add them to the spread. I fill the rest of the table with sour cream and different kinds of salsa. It's a very impressive-looking table, and the best part is that your guests can customize their quesadillas to their liking and grill them up themselves. There's very little work for you and everyone's happy. Carnivores, vegetarians, and picky eaters alike will love this.

1½ pounds chicken thighs, boneless, skinless

1½ pounds skirt steak

Kosher salt and freshly ground black pepper, to taste

2 ears corn, shucked

2 cups cheddar cheese, shredded

2 cups pepper jack cheese, shredded

1 14-ounce can black beans, rinsed and drained

1 bunch scallions, sliced

20 large flour tortillas, 10 inches each

FOR THE GARNISH:

1 cup sour cream

1 avocado, peeled, pitted, and diced

1 lime, zested

Salt

1 cup salsa, store-bought

8–12 lime wedges, to serve

1 bunch cilantro, leaves only, for garnish

1. Preheat grill or grill pan over medium-high heat.

2. Season chicken and steak with salt and pepper. Place on grill and cook until lightly charred, about 4 minutes. Flip and cook another 4 minutes or until chicken is cooked through and steak is medium rare. Remove to a plate and keep warm. Thinly slice the steak and chicken thighs.

3. Place corn in a steamer basket set in a large pot with an inch of water. Bring to a boil and allow the corn to cook until tender, about 5 minutes. Remove from the steamer, then cool until able to handle. Cut the corn off the cob.

4. Place corn, cheddar cheese, pepper jack cheese, black beans, and scallions in individual bowls. Arrange a platter of sliced chicken and steak.

5. Allow guests to build their own quesadillas with desired toppings. Fold tortillas in half and place on grill to cook until golden, about 3 minutes; then flip and cook another 3 minutes or until golden and cheese is warm and melted.

FOR THE GARNISH:

6. In a small bowl, add the sour cream, avocado, lime zest, and a pinch of salt and mix to combine.

7. Serve finished quesadillas with avocado mixture, salsa, lime wedges, and cilantro in individual bowls.

Butternut Squash and Baked Ziti

Serves: 24 / **Prep Time:** 15 minutes / **Cook Time:** 20 minutes

Courtesy of Clinton Kelly / This dish is so over-the-top decadent that your friends and family will be begging you to bring it to their next potluck occasion. It's got not one, not two, not three, but five different kinds of cheeses. I mean, talk about a guilty pleasure! It kind of makes me want to draw the blinds, hop into my pajamas with a glass of white wine and a good TV show, and call it a night.

1 pound butternut squash, peeled and cut into 1-inch cubes

2 tablespoons extra-virgin olive oil

Kosher salt and freshly ground black pepper, to taste

1 pound ziti

¼ cup butter

1 yellow onion, finely chopped

2 cloves garlic, minced

3 sage leaves, chopped

¼ cup all-purpose flour

½ cup white wine

1¾ cups vegetable stock

1 teaspoon nutmeg

1½ cups fontina cheese, chopped

1½ cups Asiago cheese, grated

1½ cups Parmigiano-Reggiano, grated

8 ounces cream cheese

½ cup mozzarella cheese, shredded

1. Preheat oven to 450°F.

2. Place the cubed butternut squash on a sheet tray. Drizzle with olive oil and season with salt and pepper. Place in the oven and roast for 10 minutes. Rotate the squash with a spatula and roast for an additional 5 minutes. Remove from oven and set aside.

3. Bring a large pot of salted water to a boil. Drop the ziti into the boiling water and cook for 2 minutes less than the package directions suggest. Drain and set aside.

4. Meanwhile, melt the butter in a large Dutch oven over medium heat. Once melted, add the onion, garlic, and sage. Season with salt and pepper and sauté until vegetables are translucent (about 5 minutes). Add the flour, stir to combine, and cook for 2 minutes. Add the wine and stock and bring to a simmer. Add the nutmeg. Cook for 5 minutes to thicken the sauce and cook off the alcohol.

5. Turn the heat to low and add in all the cheeses, except the mozzarella. Stir vigorously to combine until a smooth mixture forms. Remove from heat. Add the reserved ziti and butternut squash, and season with salt and pepper to taste. Sprinkle the top with shredded mozzarella.

6. Place in the oven and broil for 2-3 minutes. Serve immediately.

Sunday Sauce with Ribs, Chicken, and Sausage

Serves: 8 / **Prep Time:** 20 minutes / **Cook Time:** 4 hours

Courtesy of Mario Batali / I have wonderful family memories of our Sunday suppers—those long leisurely meals, where no one wants to leave. We would just sit there for hours, enjoying each other's company. This dish has been on my table for many of those great dinners. It's something that I put on the stove in the morning and all day long people come by and just grab some crunchy bread and dip it in the sauce for a taste and a stir. The house fills with the most remarkable smells; the windows fog from the steam of the pasta water. It just goes to show that entertaining doesn't have to be fancy, you just need to create a space to make great conversation happen with the people you care about over delicious food.

¼ cup, plus 2 tablespoons extra-virgin olive oil

12 pork spareribs, cut into 2-inch pieces

6 chicken thighs, skin-on, bone-in

Kosher salt and freshly ground black pepper, to taste

1 red onion, finely chopped

4 cloves garlic, sliced

½ bottle dry red wine

2 28-ounce cans whole, peeled San Marzano tomatoes, crushed by hand

Small pinch of red chili flakes

1 pound sweet Italian fennel sausage

1 pound rigatoni pasta

3-4 tablespoons Pecorino Romano, freshly grated, to serve

1. In a large pasta pot or Dutch oven, add ¼ cup oil and place over medium-high heat until almost smoking. Season the ribs and chicken with salt and pepper to taste. Working in batches, sear the seasoned ribs and chicken over medium heat until dark golden brown. Remove the seared meat to a plate and set aside.

2. Add the onion and garlic to the pot and sauté, scraping the pan with a wooden spoon to loosen any brown bits. Cook until the onions are golden brown and very soft, about 10 minutes. Add the wine, tomatoes, chili flakes, browned meat, and sausages, and salt and pepper to taste.

3. Reduce the heat to a simmer and cook 2½-3 hours, stirring occasionally and skimming off the fat as necessary. Season the sauce to taste with salt and pepper.

4. Bring water to boil in a large pasta pot and season with salt. Cook rigatoni for 2 minutes less than directions on the package.

5. Toss the pasta with a few ladles of the Sunday Sauce and serve alongside the ribs, chicken, and sausage.

6. Garnish with the freshly grated Pecorino.

Stuffed Shells with Corn and Zucchini

Serves: 4–6 / Prep Time: 30 minutes / Cook Time: 1 hour

Courtesy of Michael Symon / This is a great make-ahead meal that you can really serve all year round. This version, with corn and zucchini, is something we eat around Memorial Day. I have a yearly tradition of going to play golf with my dad, Uncle DJ, and my grandfather Pap and then heading back to Uncle DJ's house for a big cookout with all of the family. This is the dish I always bring because it's easy to make and it travels so well.

1 12-ounce box large pasta shells

2 tablespoons olive oil

1½ cups fresh corn, cut off the cob, or frozen and thawed

1 cup zucchini, diced

Kosher salt and freshly ground black pepper, to taste

1 pound whole milk ricotta

2 cups fresh mozzarella, grated, divided

1½ cups freshly grated Parmigiano-Reggiano, divided

½ cup parsley, finely chopped

½ cup basil, finely chopped

FOR THE POMODORO SAUCE:

¼ cup extra-virgin olive oil

1 small onion, peeled and finely diced, about 1 cup

2 cloves garlic, peeled and minced

Kosher salt and freshly ground black pepper, to taste

¼ teaspoon chili flakes

1 small bunch fresh oregano, tied with kitchen twine

1 28-ounce can whole peeled tomatoes, crushed by hand

1 bunch basil, torn, to garnish

1. Preheat oven to 375°F.

2. Bring a large pot of salted water to a boil and cook the pasta until al dente, according to package directions.

3. In a medium sauté pan, add olive oil and heat over medium-high heat. Add corn and zucchini, season with salt and pepper, and cook until almost tender, about 4-5 minutes. Remove to a bowl to cool to room temperature.

4. In a large bowl, add the ricotta, 1 cup mozzarella, 1 cup Parmigiano-Reggiano, corn, zucchini, parsley, and basil, and season with salt and pepper.

5. In a 9 x 9 casserole dish, add a layer of pomodoro sauce. Fill each cooked shell with some of the cheese mixture and place in the dish, seam-side up. Cover the shells with another layer of pomodoro sauce. Top with remaining mozzarella and Parmigiano-Reggiano.

6. Loosely cover with aluminum foil and bake for 30 minutes. Uncover and bake for another 10 minutes, until light golden brown and bubbly. Remove and let cool for 10 minutes before serving.

FOR THE POMODORO SAUCE:

7. Place a medium saucepan over medium heat and add olive oil. Add the onions and garlic and season with salt. Sauté until translucent, about 8–10 minutes. Add chili flakes, bundle of oregano, and tomatoes, and season with salt and pepper. Bring to a simmer, reduce heat to medium-low, and cook for 30 minutes. Remove from heat.

8. Remove oregano and discard. Using an immersion blender, puree until smooth. Add basil and stir to combine.

Perfect Roasted Chicken

Serves: 4 / **Prep Time:** 30 minutes / **Inactive Time:** 2 hours / **Cook Time:** 1 hour

Courtesy of Mario Batali / Julia Child always said that you can judge the quality of a restaurant and the talent of the chef by the roasted chicken. It's not the style of the dish or the ingredients chosen to create the flavors, it's the care taken to create perfectly crispy skin and moist meat. I couldn't agree more and I think she would be proud of the beautiful bird in this recipe. Brining your chicken ensures that the meat stays very moist and tender and flavors the bird throughout. I pat the skin dry and roast it with simple herbs and aromatics to create what I think is the perfect balance of flavor. I hope you like it as much as I do.

FOR THE BRINE:

1 cup kosher salt

1 stick cinnamon

1 bunch fresh rosemary

½ cup apple cider

2 quarts boiling water

2 quarts ice

FOR THE CHICKEN:

1 2½- to 3-pound free-range chicken

3 tablespoons extra-virgin olive oil

2 tablespoons kosher salt

2 tablespoons freshly ground black pepper

1 lemon, thinly sliced

1 bunch fresh thyme

8 cloves garlic

6 sprigs fresh marjoram

1 small red onion, thinly sliced

FOR THE BRINE:

1. In a plastic container or stainless steel bowl large enough to hold the chicken, stir the salt, cinnamon, rosemary, and cider together. Pour in the boiling water and stir to dissolve. Add the ice and stir to chill. Submerge the chicken in the brine.

2. Place a plate on top of the bird to prevent it from floating. The chicken should be completely submerged throughout the brining process. Cover and refrigerate for 1 hour. Pour off the brine and dry the chicken thoroughly with paper towels. Place the brined bird on a plate and put in the refrigerator to air-dry, uncovered, for at least another hour before roasting.

FOR THE CHICKEN:

3. Preheat the oven to 475°F.

4. Remove the chicken from the refrigerator and let stand at room temperature for 30 minutes.

5. Rub the whole chicken with olive oil. In a small bowl, mix the salt and pepper and season the chicken inside and out with the mixture. Place 1 slice of lemon under the skin and in the center of each breast. Place the thyme, garlic, marjoram, remaining lemon slices, and onion in the chicken's cavity.

6. Place the chicken on a rack set inside a roasting pan. Roast the chicken for 1 hour. Cook the chicken until the thigh juices run clear and an instant-read thermometer inserted into the thickest part of the thigh, away from the bone, registers 160°F. Transfer the chicken to a warmed platter in a warm place and let rest for 10–15 minutes. Carve and serve.

Corned Beef "Hash" Casserole

Serves: 6–8 / **Prep Time:** 10 minutes / **Inactive Time:** 12 hours / **Cook Time:** 1 hour, 30 minutes

Courtesy of Michael Symon / Back in the day, they used to call me the "Casserole King of Cleveland." Well, actually they didn't, but I'm working on getting that title to stick. And I think that this corned beef hash casserole is the one to do it. This dish combines two of my favorite indulgent breakfasts: corned beef hash and bread pudding. I like to assemble this dish the night before and let it soak overnight in the fridge so that when you bake it, it comes out kind of like a soufflé with a crunchy top. I get so excited that I wake up really early in the morning, while everyone else is still sleeping, and pop this bad boy in the oven so that its aroma draws the family out of their beds and into the kitchen, my favorite room in the house.

FOR THE CARAMELIZED ONIONS:

2 onions, sliced

2 tablespoons extra-virgin olive oil

Kosher salt and freshly ground black pepper, to taste

FOR THE CASSEROLE:

1½-pound challah, brioche, or pullman loaf, crusts trimmed

⅓ pound corned beef, shaved

4 cups Gruyère, shredded

½ cup chives, chopped

½ cup fresh parsley, chopped

8 large eggs

4 cups whole milk

2 tablespoons whole-grain mustard

1 tablespoon kosher salt

1 tablespoon chili flakes

1 tablespoon black pepper

FOR THE CARAMELIZED ONIONS:

1. Place a large sauté pan over medium-low heat. Add olive oil and onions. Season with salt and pepper and cook until golden, about 25 minutes.

FOR THE CASSEROLE:

2. Slice bread into long slices, about ⅓-inch thick. You should have 6 or 7 slices. Arrange 3 of the slices in one layer in a buttered casserole dish. Top with half the corned beef. Cover with half the cheese, the onions, and half the herbs. Top with 3 more slices of bread (it doesn't matter if the bread doesn't fit snugly, although you can use an extra slice to fill in any gaps). Arrange the remaining Gruyère and herbs over the bread.

3. In a mixing bowl, whisk eggs until combined. Add milk, mustard, salt, and pepper and whisk until light and frothy. Pour egg mixture evenly over the bread. Cover with plastic wrap and refrigerate overnight.

4. When ready to bake, preheat the oven to 350°F. Bake the casserole on the bottom rack for 1½ hours until puffed and browned. Let rest for 15 minutes before cutting into squares.

Oven Fried Chicken

Serves: 8 / **Prep Time:** 5 minutes / **Cook Time:** 1 hour, 15 minutes

Courtesy of Clinton Kelly / Do you sometimes feel like swimsuit season is always right around the corner? You're not alone. I try to eat a healthy and balanced diet, but I still get cravings for classic comfort dishes like fried chicken. And if I deprive myself by only eating carrot sticks and celery, I get *hangry*: you know, hungry with a splash of anger. That's why I created this recipe: so I could enjoy the crunch and flavors of fried chicken but without feeling too guilty. It's delicious, and the best part is that you're going to look good while you eat it, too.

Olive oil spray

1 cup nonfat Greek yogurt

1 tablespoon honey

1 tablespoon hot sauce

2 cups crushed cornflakes

2 teaspoons dried oregano

2 teaspoons dried thyme

Kosher salt and freshly cracked black pepper, to taste

4 chicken thighs, bone-in, skin-on

2 chicken breasts, bone-in, skin-on, split

1. Preheat oven to 350°F.

2. Prepare a baking sheet with a cooling rack inside and coat with olive oil spray.

3. In a large bowl, whisk together the yogurt, honey, and hot sauce. Season with salt and pepper.

4. In another rimmed baking dish or bowl, stir together the cornflakes, oregano, and thyme. Season with salt and pepper.

5. Working one piece at a time, coat chicken in the yogurt mixture. Dredge in the cornflakes mixture, pressing with your hands to coat completely. Gently place chicken on the prepared baking sheet and repeat with remaining pieces.

6. Spray the chicken with olive oil and bake for 1 hour. Remove white pieces of chicken and continue to bake the dark meat for 15 more minutes, or until all the chicken registers 165°F on an instant-read thermometer.

7. Allow chicken to cool slightly before serving.

Eye of Round Roast

Serves: 10–12 / **Prep Time:** 5 minutes / **Inactive Time:** Overnight / **Cook Time:** 1 hour, 15 minutes

Courtesy of Michael Symon / This dish is a great substitute for prime rib or beef tenderloin, or any of those more expensive cuts of beef. It's a dish that is really impressive visually, but it won't break the bank. And with only six ingredients, you'll have this in the oven in five minutes flat. After that you just have to check on it every so often and baste it with those delicious juices. It's so easy and great to feed a crowd any night of the week. I like to serve this dish with my Mashed Potato Casserole (page 147).

1 4-pound eye round roast, tied

Kosher salt and freshly cracked black pepper, to taste

Extra-virgin olive oil

4 sprigs rosemary

4 garlic cloves, unpeeled, smashed

1. Liberally season the eye round roast with salt and pepper and refrigerate overnight.

2. 1 hour before cooking, remove the roast from the refrigerator and allow to come to room temperature.

3. Preheat oven to 400°F.

4. Rub the roast with olive oil and drizzle olive oil onto the bottom of the roasting pan.

5. Add the garlic and rosemary to the pan and place the roast on top.

6. Cook for 30 minutes and then baste the roast with any pan drippings.

7. Reduce heat to 350°F and cook until the meat is medium rare (an internal temperature of 125–130°F), about 1 hour and 15 minutes.

8. Keep basting the roast every 30 minutes until it is done. (Keep in mind that the roast will continue to cook while resting.)

9. Remove the roast from the oven and put it on a cutting board to rest, uncovered, for 20 minutes. Slice the roast to the desired thickness and serve.

Carla's Broccoli Gratin

Serves: 8–10 / **Prep Time:** 15 minutes / **Cook Time:** 40 minutes

Courtesy of Carla Hall / Every Thanksgiving table has some sort of creamy vegetable casserole; whether it's green bean or squash, creamed spinach or corn, you've just got to have it. In my house it's broccoli. I blanch fresh broccoli and fold it into a cheesy base before I cover it in bread crumbs and bake it. But you could totally use frozen broccoli to get it in the oven even faster. Anything you need to do to get through the holiday . . . I approve!

2 large bunches of broccoli, approximately 3 pounds of florets

5 tablespoons butter

4 tablespoons all-purpose flour

4 cups milk

2 teaspoons salt

1 teaspoon chopped fresh thyme

¼ teaspoon freshly grated nutmeg

1⅓ cups grated Gruyère cheese

⅓ cup dry, seasoned bread crumbs

¼ teaspoon ground black pepper

1. Preheat oven to 375°F. Butter a 9 x 13 baking dish and set aside.

2. Steam the broccoli florets in a large pot of boiling water fitted with a steamer basket for 5-7 minutes, until the florets are just tender. Rinse them in cold water, drain, and arrange them in a single layer in the buttered dish.

3. In a large saucepan over medium heat, melt the butter and whisk in the flour until it forms a smooth paste. Continue whisking, cook for about 2 minutes, and then gradually— ⅓ cup at a time—add the milk. Continue whisking and cook until the sauce is completely heated through, smooth, and thickened. Remove from heat and season with salt, thyme, and nutmeg. This is the béchamel sauce.

4. Pour 2 cups of the béchamel sauce over the steamed broccoli and gently toss the florets to make sure they are thoroughly coated with the sauce.

5. Bake uncovered for 15 minutes. Stir together the grated Gruyère cheese and bread crumbs and sprinkle them over the broccoli. Bake for an additional 10-15 minutes, until the broccoli gratin is hot and bubbly and the cheese is melted and browned. Sprinkle the surface of the baked gratin with the ground pepper and serve hot.

Carla's Sticky Pork Ribs

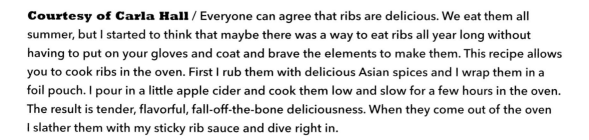

Serves: 12 / **Prep Time:** 15 minutes / **Cook Time:** 1 hour, 30 minutes

Courtesy of Carla Hall / Everyone can agree that ribs are delicious. We eat them all summer, but I started to think that maybe there was a way to eat ribs all year long without having to put on your gloves and coat and brave the elements to make them. This recipe allows you to cook ribs in the oven. First I rub them with delicious Asian spices and I wrap them in a foil pouch. I pour in a little apple cider and cook them low and slow for a few hours in the oven. The result is tender, flavorful, fall-off-the-bone deliciousness. When they come out of the oven I slather them with my sticky rib sauce and dive right in.

1 tablespoon garlic powder

1 tablespoon onion powder

1 tablespoon Chinese five-spice powder

2 teaspoons granulated sugar

2 teaspoons kosher salt

2 slabs of baby back ribs

¼ cup apple cider vinegar

FOR THE STICKY SAUCE:

Vegetable oil

1 small yellow onion or 1 large shallot, finely chopped

2 garlic cloves, minced

1 tablespoon fresh ginger, minced

¼ cup low-sodium soy sauce

¼ cup brown sugar

¼ cup ketchup

2 tablespoons honey

1 tablespoon sesame oil

1 tablespoon chili sauce

2 tablespoons sriracha

1. Preheat oven to 350°F.

2. In a small bowl, stir together the spices, sugar, and salt. Rub the ribs with the mixture, making sure to coat completely. Place the ribs on a large piece of foil and fold to form a seam along the top and edges. Bake for 40 minutes. Carefully open the foil and pour in the apple cider. Reseal the foil and continue to bake for 45 more minutes.

3. Serve with the sauce.

FOR THE STICKY SAUCE:

4. Heat a large saucepan over medium heat with a few tablespoons of vegetable oil. Sauté the onion until translucent, about 2 minutes, then add the garlic and ginger and cook until fragrant. Add the remaining ingredients except the sriracha and stir to combine. Bring mixture to a boil and reduce to a simmer. Cook for 5 minutes or until sauce has thickened.

5. Remove from heat, stir in sriracha, and allow all to cool until ready to serve. Sauce can be made up to a week in advance and stored in the fridge.

Red Wine Braised Brisket

Serves: 8 / **Prep Time:** 5 minutes / **Cook Time:** 1 hour

Courtesy of Mario Batali / This is one of those dishes that holds up so well in the freezer that when I make this recipe, I often prepare two briskets at a time and freeze one for another occasion. Sometimes I make it to eat alongside creamy polenta or mashed potatoes. But other times I shred the whole thing and serve it with pasta or pile it high on a potato roll. However you choose to serve it, this is a winning recipe that won't disappoint your friends and family.

6 tablespoons extra-virgin olive oil

1 4-pound beef brisket

Kosher salt and freshly ground black pepper, to taste

2 Spanish onions, diced

1 carrot, cut into ½-inch rounds

2 celery stalks, cut into ½-inch-thick slices

4 ounces pancetta, diced

2 cups Barolo or other hearty red wine

2 cups store-bought tomato sauce

FOR THE GREMOLATA:

⅓ cup parsley, chopped

Zest of 2 lemons

Kosher salt and freshly ground black pepper, to taste

1. In a large Dutch oven, heat the olive oil over high heat until smoking. Season the meat liberally with salt and pepper.

2. Sear in the pan for 4–5 minutes per side until golden brown. Remove to a plate.

3. Add the onions, carrot, celery, and pancetta and cook until the vegetables are light brown and starting to soften, about 8 minutes.

4. Add the wine and tomato sauce and bring to a boil. Add the brisket and its juices back to the pan and reduce to a simmer. Cook until the meat is very tender, 3½–4 hours.

5. Remove the brisket to a platter.

FOR THE GREMOLATA:

6. Combine the chopped parsley, lemon zest, salt, and pepper. Sprinkle over top of the sliced brisket and serve.

Mashed Potato Casserole

Serves: 6–8 / **Prep Time:** 15 minutes / **Cook Time:** 1 hour

Courtesy of Michael Symon / Sometimes entertaining can become stressful. I find that people get really overwhelmed when they have a lot of last-minute cooking to do as their guests arrive. So I decided to create this mashed potato recipe that allows you to make it in advance and put it in a casserole dish the day before. Then when your friends or family arrive for the big event you just top it with crunchy bread crumbs and fresh herbs and bake it in the oven. The outcome is just as creamy and delicious as the classic mash but without all the stress that can come with last-minute mixing and stirring.

5 pounds Yukon Gold potatoes, peeled

1 stick butter, room temperature

1 cup sour cream

Kosher salt and freshly ground black pepper, to taste

FOR THE TOPPING:

1½ cups panko bread crumbs

1 tablespoon fresh flat-leaf parsley, chopped

1 tablespoon fresh dill, chopped

1 tablespoon fresh grated or prepared horseradish

1 lemon, zested

1 tablespoon extra-virgin olive oil

Kosher salt and freshly ground black pepper, to taste

1. Preheat oven to 400°F.

2. In a large pot of salted water, add the potatoes and bring to a boil. Lower the heat slightly and cook until the potatoes are tender, about 25-30 minutes. Reserve 1 cup of the starchy potato water. Remove from heat. Drain the potatoes and place back in the pot.

3. In a small saucepan, melt the butter and sour cream and stir to combine. Pour over the cooked and drained potatoes in the warm pot, and mash while slowly adding some of the reserved potato water to get the right softness and consistency. Keep the mixture loose; it will thicken on standing and reheating. Add salt and pepper to taste.

4. Add the potato mixture to a buttered 9 x 13 baking dish.

FOR THE TOPPING:

5. In a bowl, add the panko, parsley, dill, horseradish, and lemon zest, then mix to combine. Stir in the olive oil and season with salt and pepper. Top the mashed potatoes with the bread crumb mixture. Bake for 30 minutes.

Entertaining in an Instant

Okay, so you're throwing a fabulous dinner party for your closest friends. Your home is immaculate, your wine is perfectly chilled, the food is exquisitely seasoned—but, ugh, you still have to decorate the table. We know what you're thinking: how do you style that table in a thoughtful way that will shine and dazzle your guests without breaking the bank? Like this, of course!

Clinton Kelly: When I throw a party, whenever possible, I like to create centerpieces that are also party favors. During the summer when I have a barbecue, I buy young potted herbs; then I wrap the pots in a little bit of fabric or a napkin, something like burlap or gingham, and tie it with rope just below the lip of each pot. Then I line the table with this elegant row of summer herbs, which let off a lovely aroma.

Mario Batali: At my parties, I let the food be the star. I like to fill my table with all kinds of little bites of food to help my guests settle in, and I just arrange everything in a way that looks beautiful. Little cups of coarse sea salt, some marinated olives floating in olive oil, maybe some fresh figs and prosciutto; perhaps some radishes with good olive oil, chickpeas tossed with tapenade, some sliced bread, even pickles, strategically placed across the table to create a very calculated yet effortless vibe that invites your guests to sit, eat, drink, and enjoy.

Michael Symon: Every year Liz and I throw a Christmas party with our dearest friends. We like to collect ornaments that we use as placeholders for the seating arrangements. We use the ornaments as napkin rings and lay them out on the plates of our guests. Write your guests' names and the date of your party on the bottoms of the ornaments. At the end of the party, they get to take their placeholder home with them as a party favor. And every year, as they decorate for the holidays, they will reminisce about how much fun they had at your party.

Carla Hall: You don't have to go crazy trying to set the table with a ton of fresh flowers or fancy candles. Sometimes the best ideas are the easiest. I love a pucker, so I often decorate with lemons. I find that something as simple as a rectangular wooden bowl or silver tray with lemons artfully arranged down the length of the table can be so gorgeous in its simplicity. Then, at the end of the party, I like to leave a goody bag for each of my guests with a handwritten recipe for lemonade attached. They fill their bag with all those lemons you bought and head home for some homemade goodness.

Chapter 4

Last-Minute Meals

When you're trying to balance work with picking up the kids from school, or coaching the basketball team, it can feel like there aren't enough hours in the day to get a delicious meal on the table. It's almost like the second you walk in the door, everybody's hungry and about to fall apart. It's enough to make you want to hit the drive-through. Fight that urge, because here we have put together a ton of easy recipes that you can have on your dinner table in less than twenty minutes, start to finish. We always do our best to teach you not only how to follow a recipe but how to better understand which techniques will help you succeed in this endeavor. Once you've learned just a few of our tricks, you'll be able to add a little of your own flare to these tried-and-true weeknight meals, making something delicious happen every night of the week.

We've tested countless strategies over the past six years to cut your cook time down so that you'll spend less time in the kitchen and more time around the table with your family. We have recipes like microwave eggplant parmesan, a five-minute appetizer made in the toaster oven, a chilled soup with no oven required (ideal for those hot summer days), and a delicious steak for two, perfect for date night. We hope that you'll find everything you need right here to make a beautiful meal while making the most of the little time you have.

—CLINTON KELLY

Apple Pancake Rings with Apple Cider Syrup

Makes: 24 rings / **Prep Time:** 10 minutes / **Cook Time:** 5 minutes

Courtesy of Carla Hall / I remember this recipe from when I was a kid. My mother used to have one of those recipe boxes from way back, with the crazy Jell-O salads and chicken tetrazzini recipes. This recipe is inspired by something that I'm sure came out of that collection. It's so simple and easy and a great way to get the kids into the kitchen with you in the mornings for some fun. I made this recipe even easier by calling for your favorite pancake mix, but if you have a pancake recipe that you love, feel free to use it.

1 cup pancake mix, your favorite

1 egg

½ cup milk

1 teaspoon pumpkin pie spice

Zest of half a lemon

3 Granny Smith apples, peeled and cored

2 tablespoons butter

FOR THE APPLE CIDER SYRUP:

2 cups apple cider

Zest and juice of half a lemon

1 pinch ground cinnamon

1. In a large bowl, add pancake mix, egg, and milk, and whisk until smooth. Add pumpkin pie spice and the zest of half a lemon. Mix to combine. Set aside.

2. Cut apples crosswise in ⅛-inch slices.

3. Preheat griddle or nonstick pan over medium-high heat. Add a tablespoon of butter at a time to grease the griddle, or use cooking spray. Using a toothpick or 2 forks, dip apple slices into batter. Place slices on the griddle and cook until golden brown. Flip and cook on the other side until golden brown. Serve hot with Apple Cider Syrup.

FOR THE APPLE CIDER SYRUP:

4. Add apple cider, lemon zest and juice, and cinnamon to a saucepan and bring to a boil. Reduce the liquid by half, to a syrupy consistency. Set aside to cool.

Black Bean and Egg Tacos

Serves: 6 / **Prep Time:** 5 minutes / **Cook Time:** 10 minutes

Courtesy of Mario Batali / This is a great morning meal for the whole family because you can have it on the table in fifteen minutes. It's also jam-packed with protein and fiber, so it keeps you full for hours and hours. As you know, this Mexican flavor combination is one of my all-time favorites; and I'm pretty sure that you've got all of these ingredients right inside that fridge of yours right now. So what are you waiting for? Get in there and get cooking!

1 can black beans, drained and rinsed

6 eggs, beaten

1 bunch scallions, thinly sliced, greens and whites separated

Kosher salt and freshly ground black pepper, to taste

1 tablespoon extra-virgin olive oil

Hot sauce, to taste

½ cup cheddar cheese, shredded

12 corn tortillas, warmed

1. In a large mixing bowl, add black beans, eggs, scallion whites, and a pinch of salt and pepper. Mix to combine.

2. Add oil to a skillet and place over medium-high heat. Add the bean and egg mixture. Using a rubber spatula, stir and cook until the eggs are softly scrambled. Remove from heat. Add a couple dashes of hot sauce and the cheese. Stir to melt the cheese.

3. Divide the egg and bean mixture evenly among the warmed tortillas. Garnish with scallion greens and serve.

Kale Hummus Flatbreads

Serves: 4–6 / **Prep Time:** 15 minutes / **Cook Time:** 20 minutes

Courtesy of Carla Hall / This is one of those meals that I developed for the weeknights when you get home and you want to eat something nutritious, but you just can't muster up the energy to cook. This dish is really healthy, but it also utilizes all of those shortcuts that we look for at the grocery store. I use prewashed and pre-chopped kale, served with flatbread and a little hummus that I jazz up with some lemon juice and some fresh herbs. Then I grill it up, and in no time at all I have fast food that I feel good about.

2 tablespoons extra-virgin olive oil

1 small red onion, peeled and finely diced

1 8-ounce bag chopped kale

¼ cup chicken stock

1 tablespoon red wine vinegar

1 teaspoon red chili flakes

Kosher salt and freshly ground black pepper, to taste

FOR THE HUMMUS:

1 container store-bought hummus

Zest and juice of 1 lemon

¼ cup parsley leaves, chopped

2 tablespoons chives, chopped

Kosher salt and freshly ground black pepper, to taste

6 pocketless pita bread

2 tablespoons extra-virgin olive oil

1. In a large sauté pan, heat olive oil on high. Add red onion and cook until almost tender, about 4 minutes. Add kale and allow to cook until slightly wilted, about 3 minutes. Add chicken stock, vinegar, and chili flakes and allow to cook until wilted, about 4–5 minutes. Season with salt and pepper.

FOR THE HUMMUS:

2. In a medium bowl, add the store-bought hummus, lemon zest, lemon juice, parsley, and chives and mix to combine. Season with salt and pepper if necessary.

3. Preheat grill or grill pan to medium heat. Brush both sides of pita with olive oil and place on grill. Allow to cook until charred and warmed through, about 2 minutes per side.

4. Remove pita to a plate or platter, spread hummus on top of each pita, and top with kale to serve.

Deviled Cheese Toasts

Serves: 6 / **Prep Time:** 5 minutes / **Cook Time:** 2–4 minutes

Courtesy of Clinton Kelly / I'm obsessed with this recipe. Talk about fab on the fly! This dish comes together in about five minutes and you can make it in your toaster oven. That means when you get that last-minute call that someone's dropping by with a nice bottle of sauvignon blanc and some good conversation, you've got just the thing to whip up in a flash that no one could possibly refuse.

6 slices crusty Italian bread, thinly sliced

½ pound cheddar cheese, grated

1 cup mayonnaise

¼ cup dill pickles, chopped

¼ cup roasted red bell pepper, chopped

1 pinch red chili flakes

1. Preheat oven or toaster oven to broil.

2. Lightly toast bread (about 30 seconds). Remove and set aside.

3. Combine the cheddar cheese, mayonnaise, pickles, roasted peppers, and chili flakes in a bowl. Spread a thick layer of the mixture onto each bread slice. Place under the broiler until golden brown and bubbly on top, about 2-4 minutes.

Ajo Verde

Serves: 4 / **Prep Time:** 15 minutes

Courtesy of Mario Batali / I make this dish all the time in the hot summer months because all you need to bring the delicious Spanish flavors together is a blender. In Spain, this soup is traditionally called *ajo blanco* because it's white in color. This version keeps the cucumber skins on and, with the addition of a jalapeño, takes on a beautiful pale-green hue. I love the complexity of the flavors in this soup. Serve it as a first course or pour it in little espresso cups or shot glasses and serve with appetizers at your next summertime soiree.

2½ cups stale crusty bread, crust removed

½ cup blanched whole almonds

1 cup ice water

2 cups green grapes, plus additional halved grapes for garnish

2 English cucumbers, roughly chopped

2 cloves garlic, peeled

2 tablespoons sherry vinegar

½ cup extra-virgin olive oil, plus additional to garnish

Kosher salt and freshly ground black pepper, to taste

1 jalapeño, thinly sliced, to garnish

1. In a medium bowl, add bread, almonds, and ice water and allow to soak for 5 minutes, until the bread is soft.

2. In the carafe of a blender, add grapes, cucumbers, garlic, soaked bread, and almonds. Blend until smooth and season with salt and pepper.

3. With the blender running, add the vinegar and olive oil, then blend until emulsified.

4. Divide among 4 bowls. Garnish with additional grape halves, jalapeño slices, and a drizzle of olive oil.

Brie and Apple Grilled Cheese

Serves: 4 / **Prep Time:** 5 minutes / **Cook Time:** 5 minutes

Courtesy of Clinton Kelly / Obviously a grilled cheese sandwich is a classic quick-fix dinner when you're in a pinch. I know that it's easy to find yourself in a dinner rut, so I came up with this recipe to add some excitement to your dinner table and up your grilled cheese game. Brie and apples are such a great autumn combination, and I find that when melted, Brie is the perfect cheese for a sandwich. The tart apple helps to balance out the richness of the cheese. And what gourmet grilled cheese would be complete without bacon? In my house, none!

8 slices pullman loaf bread

2 tablespoons butter

¼ cup honey mustard

½ pound Brie cheese, thinly sliced

2 Granny Smith apples, cored and thinly sliced

8 slices cooked bacon or turkey bacon

1. Preheat nonstick pan or griddle over medium heat.

2. Divide bread into pairs for 4 sandwiches. Spread butter on the outside of each piece of bread. Spread the insides of the bread with ½ tablespoon of honey mustard and top with 2 slices of Brie. For each sandwich, place 3 slices of apple on 1 piece of bread and 2 slices of bacon on the other piece. Sandwich the 2 halves together.

3. Place each sandwich in a pan or on the griddle and cook until golden brown, about 3 minutes. Flip and allow the other side to cook until golden brown and cheese has melted, about 3 minutes. Remove to a plate, slice in half diagonally, and serve warm.

Sausage and Pepper Hero

Serves: 4 / **Prep Time:** 20 minutes / **Cook Time:** 20 minutes

Courtesy of Mario Batali / It's a tradition in my family that we eat these porky sandwiches at the official start to March Madness. We've been doing it for years and I find that this meal is the perfect game-day feast because it's really filling. Also, I am a firm believer that a game-day dish must be eaten with one hand, so that you can safely root for your team with the other and occasionally sip your suds without ever having to put down your sandwich. Game-day grubbing is a sport in itself.

2 tablespoons extra-virgin olive oil

1 tablespoon butter

2 red onions, cut into ¼-inch dice

2 red bell peppers, cut into ¼-inch dice

2 yellow bell peppers, cut into ¼-inch dice

1 clove garlic, finely minced

2 tablespoons balsamic vinegar

Kosher salt and freshly ground black pepper, to taste

4 sweet and/or hot Italian sausages

4 hero rolls, toasted

8 thin slices provolone cheese

FOR THE PEPERONATA:

1. Heat the oil and butter in a large skillet over medium-high heat. Add the onions and peppers and cook over high heat for 4 minutes. Stir in the minced garlic and cook on high for 30 seconds. Add balsamic vinegar and remove from heat and season with salt and pepper.

FOR THE HEROS:

2. Preheat a grill or grill pan on medium-high heat. Cook the sausages, turning as they brown on each side, until they are cooked through, about 12 minutes. Remove sausages from heat. While sausage is still hot, top with two overlapped slices of provolone.

3. Place sausage into toasted bun and top with the peperonata to serve.

Grilled Chicken with Green Goddess Dressing

Serves: 4 / Prep Time: 5 minutes / Cook Time: 10 minutes

Courtesy of Clinton Kelly / Do you want to know what I love most about this dish? It's that when you're eating it, you don't feel like you're eating a salad. It's really flavorful from the fresh herbs, and rich and creamy from the buttermilk and yogurt. For this recipe, we just toss everything into a big bowl and bathe it in that green goddess dressing and you're ready to dig right in. But if you want to jazz it up a bit and give it a more elegant presentation, toss everything but the lettuce together and serve on top of a big leaf of lettuce. It's just a little more thoughtful and perfect for a crowd.

FOR THE CHICKEN THIGHS:

4 boneless, skinless chicken thighs

2 tablespoons extra-virgin olive oil

Kosher salt and freshly ground black pepper, to taste

FOR THE GREEN GODDESS DRESSING:

⅓ cup Greek yogurt

3 tablespoons buttermilk

3 tablespoons chives, roughly chopped

3 tablespoons parsley, leaves only

3 tablespoons tarragon, leaves only

1 lemon, juiced

1 anchovy filet

1 clove garlic, peeled and minced

Kosher salt and freshly ground black pepper, to taste

2 pints cherry tomatoes, halved

1 English cucumber, thinly sliced

1 small red onion, peeled and small diced

1 avocado, pitted and diced

1 head Bibb lettuce, leaves torn

FOR THE CHICKEN THIGHS:

1. Preheat a grill pan over medium-high heat. Brush chicken with olive oil and season with kosher salt and freshly ground black pepper. Place on the grill and cook, undisturbed, about 4 minutes; flip and continue to grill until cooked through, another 4 minutes. Remove to a plate and keep warm.

FOR THE GREEN GODDESS DRESSING:

2. In the bowl of a food processor, add the Greek yogurt, buttermilk, chives, parsley, tarragon, lemon juice, anchovy, and garlic. Pulse to combine. Season with salt and pepper.

3. Add the cherry tomatoes, English cucumber, red onion, and avocado to a large bowl. Add green goddess dressing and torn lettuce. Toss to combine. Season with salt and freshly ground black pepper. Top with the grilled chicken and serve.

Microwaved Eggplant Parmesan

Serves: 4 / **Prep Time:** 15 minutes / **Cook Time:** 15 minutes

Courtesy of Michael Symon / A viewer once wrote in to ask if there was any way to make eggplant parmesan in the microwave. I had never tried since I'm not really a microwaving kind of guy, but I figured it out, and you know what? This recipe is delicious. You definitely save yourself some calories by not frying the eggplant in oil, not to mention all the time you save by using a microwave. And the cleanup is a cinch.

¾ cup panko bread crumbs

½ cup freshly grated Parmigiano-Reggiano

1 large Italian eggplant, peeled and sliced ½-inch thick

Kosher salt and freshly ground black pepper, to taste

¼ cup olive oil

1½ cups store-bought tomato sauce

1 cup whole milk ricotta

1 cup fresh mozzarella, thinly sliced

¼ cup basil leaves, torn

1. Preheat the oven to 350°F.

2. Combine the panko and Parmigiano-Reggiano and spread into an even layer on a sheet tray. Bake for 8–10 minutes until golden brown and toasted. Make sure you check the panko after about 5 minutes, moving the edges in and the center out for even toasting. Set aside.

3. Arrange the eggplant slices in a single layer on a paper towel–lined microwave safe plate. Season with salt and pepper. Cover with another paper towel. Microwave on high for 3 minutes. Work in batches to cook all the eggplant.

4. Brush the cooked eggplant slices with olive oil and arrange on a plate in a single layer. Seal the plate with plastic wrap. Microwave again on high, about 4 minutes. Repeat with remaining eggplant.

5. Spoon ⅓ of the tomato sauce into the bottom of an 8 x 8 glass pan. Layer 4 slices of eggplant, followed by some ricotta, then mozzarella and basil. Season the cheese very lightly with salt, then repeat the process 2 more times, ending with sauce on top. Top with the toasted Parmesan panko and microwave on high, until the cheese is melted and bubbly, about 5–6 minutes.

Zucchini Spaghetti with Arugula Pesto

Serves: 4 / Prep Time: 10 minutes **/ Cook Time:** 10 minutes

Courtesy of Clinton Kelly / If you're like me, you are always looking for delicious food that's good for you; and if you can shave off some calories here and there, well, you'll save yourself some time on the treadmill. This dish is just under two hundred calories a serving. Can you believe it? And it's very simple to put together. I make this all the time in the summer when it's just too hot for a heavy bowl of pasta. Served at room temperature, this makes a great addition to a picnic or a quick and easy weeknight dinner.

1½ cups arugula

1½ cups basil leaves

⅓ cup walnuts

2 garlic cloves, smashed

½ cup grated Parmigiano-Reggiano

Extra-virgin olive oil

Kosher salt and freshly ground black pepper, to taste

3 zucchini, cut to resemble spaghetti

Panko bread crumbs, toasted, to garnish

1. Place the arugula, basil, walnuts, garlic, and cheese in a food processor and pulse. Slowly drizzle in olive oil and pulse until the mixture resembles a coarse paste. Season with salt and pepper to taste.

2. Preheat a large skillet over medium-high heat with a few tablespoons of olive oil. Add the zucchini and toss to coat in oil.

3. Add a few tablespoons of pesto and toss with the zucchini. Once the zucchini begins to take on color, transfer to a platter and top with the toasted panko to taste.

4. Serve warm or at room temperature.

NOTE: You may cut the zucchini with a spiralizer or a mandolin fitted with a julienne attachment, or shave it thin with a peeler.

Cauliflower "Risotto"

Serves: 6 / **Prep Time:** 10 minutes / **Cook Time:** 15 minutes

Courtesy of Carla Hall / This is a great low-carb dish that works really well as a side dish or a vegetarian entrée. It's so packed with flavor that you don't really even miss the carbs. Traditionally, risotto is made with a slow-cooking, short-grain rice that requires a ton of effort and basically keeps you tied to the stove, afraid to move, for hours at a time. Well, not my cauliflower version. Nope, mine takes just minutes for the cauliflower to absorb all of that great flavor.

¼ cup extra-virgin olive oil, plus more to finish

1 cup onion, diced

Kosher salt and freshly ground black pepper, to taste

1 head cauliflower, grated or cut into ¼-inch pieces

2 cloves garlic, chopped

¼ cup dry white wine

½ to 1 cup chicken stock

¼ cup heavy cream

2 teaspoons lemon zest

¼ cup toasted pine nuts

¼ cup freshly grated Parmigiano-Reggiano

2 tablespoons parsley, chopped

1. Preheat the oil in a large, high-sided sauté pan over medium heat.

2. Add the onion, season with salt and pepper, and sauté until translucent. To the same pan, add the cauliflower and the garlic, and season with salt and pepper. Sauté for 2 more minutes.

3. Deglaze the pan with white wine and cook, stirring constantly, until the liquid is almost evaporated. Add the chicken stock and heavy cream and bring to a simmer. Cook until the cauliflower is tender, about 6–8 minutes. Remove from heat and add the lemon zest, pine nuts, Parmigiano-Reggiano, parsley, and a drizzle of olive oil.

Calamari Sicilian Lifeguard Style

Serves: 4 / **Prep Time:** 10 minutes / **Cook Time:** 10 minutes

Courtesy of Mario Batali / I've never met a lifeguard from Sicily, but this is how I would imagine they cook calamari. The general rule with calamari is that you either cook it for two minutes or you cook it for an hour. If you try to eat it somewhere in between you get a chewy, rubbery mess, and nobody wants that. I find that the two-minute method works the best for a weeknight meal, and although this dish is spicy, you can really tailor the spice level to something your family can handle by switching up the peppers. This dish pairs well with some crusty Italian bread or flatbread.

1 cup Israeli couscous

1 tablespoon kosher salt

¼ cup extra-virgin olive oil

2 serrano peppers, seeded and minced

2 tablespoons pine nuts

2 tablespoons currants

1 tablespoon red pepper flakes

¼ cup capers

2 cups store-bought tomato sauce

1½ pounds cleaned calamari, tubes cut into ¼-inch rounds, tentacles halved

Kosher salt and freshly ground black pepper, to taste

3 scallions, thinly sliced

1. Bring 3 quarts of water to a boil and add 1 tablespoon of salt.

2. Cook the couscous in the boiling water for 2 minutes. Drain and rinse with cold water. Once cooled, remove and set aside to dry on a plate.

3. In a 12- to 14-inch sauté pan, heat the oil until just shimmering. Add the serranos, pine nuts, currants, and red pepper flakes and sauté until the nuts are just golden brown, about 2 minutes.

4. Add the capers, tomato sauce, and couscous and bring to a boil.

5. Add the calamari, stir to mix, and simmer for 2–3 minutes, or until the calamari is just cooked and completely opaque.

6. Season with salt and pepper, pour into a large warm bowl, sprinkle with scallions, and serve immediately.

Chicken Francese

Serves: 6 / **Prep Time:** 5 minutes / **Cook Time:** 15 minutes

Courtesy of Clinton Kelly / I'm telling you, if you make a dish and call it something in another language, all of a sudden it gets fancy. That's how I feel about this chicken dish. Really, it's just a chicken cutlet dredged in seasoned flour and egg, that is then fried and served with a lemon-and-white-wine pan sauce. And every time I go out to one of those Italian red sauce joints, I go right for this dish. Now *that's* the thing I love most about it. I would order this dish in a restaurant because it is so delicious, but it's also easy enough to make at home.

4 large chicken breasts, boneless, skinless, pounded to ½-inch thickness

Kosher salt and freshly ground black pepper, to taste

½ cup flour for dredging

4 eggs, whisked

¼ cup water

3 tablespoons extra-virgin olive oil

¾ cup white wine

¾ cup chicken stock

3 tablespoons butter

1 lemon cut into wheels, plus wedges to garnish

¼ cup fresh parsley, leaves torn

1. Season chicken with salt. Whisk together flour, salt, and pepper in a rimmed baking dish. Whisk eggs, water, salt, and pepper in a second rimmed baking dish.

2. Preheat 3 tablespoons olive oil in a large skillet over medium-high heat.

3. Working in batches to avoid overcrowding the pan, lightly coat chicken in the seasoned flour, dip in the egg mixture, and place in the oil to fry. Repeat with the remaining chicken.

4. Cook for 2-3 minutes or until golden and crispy. Flip and continue to cook on the second side until golden and crispy, about 2-3 more minutes.

5. Once chicken is cooked through, drain excess oil, and transfer to a large serving platter.

6. Remove half of the cooking oil. Deglaze the pan with the wine, making sure to scrape up any brown bits from the bottom of the pan. Stir in chicken stock and butter to emulsify. Add the lemon wheels and season with salt and pepper.

7. Remove pan from heat and add the fresh parsley.

8. Pour the sauce over the chicken, garnish with lemon wedges, and serve.

Chicken Scallopini with Tomato Mozzarella Salad

Serves: 6 / **Prep Time:** 5 minutes / **Cook Time:** 15 minutes

Courtesy of Michael Symon / This dish is so quick and easy to put together that I made it on *The Chew* for our first-ever cooking school segment. I taught eight people who had almost never cooked a meal in their lives how to make this dish. If they can get this dish on the table, think about how easy it will be for you. I love this dish because it's almost like a deconstructed chicken parmesan. I fry the cutlet as you would in the classic version, but I serve the tomatoes and basil and mozzarella on the side in a salad rather than bake the cutlets in the cheesy tomato sauce that you're used to. It just elevates the dish ever so slightly.

5 tablespoons extra-virgin olive oil, divided

2 pounds chicken breasts, boneless, skinless, pounded to ¼-inch thickness

Kosher salt and freshly ground black pepper, to taste

1½ cups flour

3 eggs

1 cup panko bread crumbs

1 cup Parmigiano-Reggiano, freshly grated

1 tablespoon red wine vinegar

½ cup cherry tomatoes, halved

½ cup bocconcini (small mozzarella balls)

½ red onion, thinly sliced

½ cup basil leaves

1 teaspoon red chili flakes, optional

1. Place a cast iron pan over medium-high heat and add about 3 tablespoons of olive oil to the pan.

2. Season the chicken with salt and pepper.

3. Place flour in a rimmed baking dish and season with salt and pepper. Whisk to combine.

4. Whisk eggs and transfer to a second rimmed baking dish. Season with salt and pepper.

5. In a third rimmed baking dish, mix the panko, Parmigiano-Reggiano, salt, and pepper.

6. Begin breading the chicken by coating lightly with the seasoned flour. Dip into the whisked eggs and then dredge in the panko mixture.

7. Gently place the breaded chicken in the hot oil and allow to cook on the first side for 3-4 minutes or until the chicken is dark golden brown.

8. Flip the chicken and continue to cook on the second side for 2-3 minutes, or until golden brown.

9. Remove to a paper towel-lined plate to drain the excess oil.

10. Meanwhile, in a medium bowl, whisk together the vinegar, remaining olive oil, salt, and pepper.

11. Add the tomatoes, bocconcini, sliced red onion, and basil. Also add chili flakes if desired. Toss in the vinaigrette to dress.

12. Plate the chicken and serve with the tomato salad.

Quick Steak au Poivre

Serves: 4 / Prep Time: 10 minutes / Cook Time: 15 minutes

Courtesy of Mario Batali / Even though this dish is quick and easy, it still feels worthy of special occasions. I think it's the perfect meal for date night because it's so impressive that your significant other will think you were in the kitchen all day long making the perfect dinner. If you're looking to score points with a certain someone special, this is the dish for you. It just might seal the deal. In that case, make sure you invite me to the wedding.

2 12-ounce boneless strip steaks

Kosher salt and freshly ground black pepper, to taste

2 tablespoons extra-virgin olive oil

1 shallot, peeled and chopped

⅓ cup brandy

2 tablespoons brined green peppercorns

1 cup beef stock

1 cup cream

1 bunch chives, sliced

1. Heat a large cast iron skillet over medium-high heat. Season the steaks generously with salt and pepper. Drizzle with olive oil. Add the steaks to the pan and sear, cooking about 3 minutes per side for medium rare.

2. Remove steaks to a plate to rest, and reduce heat to medium. Add the shallot to the pan, and cook until softened, about a minute. Very carefully add the brandy and remove the pan from the heat.

3. Using a long-stemmed lighter, ignite the brandy, allowing the alcohol to cook off. Scrape the bottom of the pan with a wooden spoon, then add the green peppercorns and stock, and bring to a boil. Stir in the cream and cook for an additional minute.

4. Slice steaks against the grain and divide among 4 plates. Stir the chives into the sauce, and spoon over the steaks to serve.

Franks 'n' Beans in a Blanket

Serves: 8 / **Prep Time:** 5 minutes / **Cook Time:** 12 minutes

Courtesy of Carla Hall / When I was growing up, my mom made "beanie weenies" for us all the time. Basically, it was just franks and beans that we would sometimes have over rice or with some toasted bread. I was looking for a quick and easy version of this that had some interesting twist the whole family would love. Just take regular old hot dogs and wrap them up in puff pastry with some mustard and some smashed baked beans. Next, top them with some crumbled bacon and bake them in the oven for about twelve minutes, and you've got a great snack or game-day treat in an instant.

1 sheet puff pastry dough, thawed

¼ cup ballpark mustard

1 16-ounce can baked beans, drained

8 all-beef hot dogs

1 egg, beaten

1 cup crumbled cooked bacon

1. Preheat oven to 350°F.

2. Cut the sheet of puff pastry into 8 rectangular pieces.

3. Evenly spread each rectangle of puff pastry with the mustard.

4. In a mixing bowl, lightly smash the baked beans. Distribute evenly among the puff pastry pieces.

5. Place one hot dog along the long edge of each rectangle and roll up the puff pastry. Place on a parchment-lined baking sheet, seam-side down. Continue with the remaining hot dogs.

6. Add a tablespoon of water to the beaten egg to create an egg wash. Brush on the tops of the puff pastry. Sprinkle with the crumbled bacon and place in the oven.

7. Bake for 10–12 minutes or until golden brown.

8. Remove and serve warm.

Ham and Turkey Cutlets with Gravy

Serves: 12 / **Prep Time:** 20 minutes / **Cook Time:** 10 minutes

Courtesy of Michael Symon / I call this my Thanksgiving saltimbocca. Saltimbocca means to jump in your mouth, and these delicious bites definitely fit the bill. Saltimbocca is an Italian dish typically made with veal and wrapped with prosciutto and sage. My version takes turkey cutlets and wraps them in Virginia ham and a little bit of sage. I dredge those in flour and sear them until crispy, and then I make a pan gravy that ties the whole dish together. It's just a slight tweak that makes this dish perfect for the holidays.

12 4-ounce turkey cutlets

24 fresh sage leaves

9 ounces thin sliced ham

Salt and freshly ground black pepper, to taste

2 tablespoons extra-virgin olive oil

3 tablespoons unsalted butter, divided

1½ cups flour

1½ teaspoons paprika

6 sprigs thyme, tied with string

3 cups low-sodium chicken stock

1. Lay the cutlets evenly spaced on a large piece of plastic wrap. Place 1–2 sage leaves on top of each cutlet, followed by 1–2 pieces of ham. Repeat with all of the cutlets, then cover them with another piece of plastic wrap. Gently pound to a ¼-inch thickness. Remove the plastic wrap, season with salt and pepper, then set aside.

2. Place a large sauté pan over medium-high heat. When the pan is hot, add 2 tablespoons of olive oil and 2 tablespoons of butter.

3. Whisk together the flour and paprika, then dredge the cutlets in the flour mixture, shaking off any excess. Add to the pan, ham-side down, and cook until golden brown, 2–3 minutes. Flip and brown on the other side, 1–2 more minutes. Remove to a platter.

4. Add the bundle of thyme to the same pan. Toast for 15–20 seconds, then add all of the chicken stock. Cook over medium-high heat, letting the stock reduce for 1–2 minutes; then add the remaining butter. Turn the heat off and whisk the butter in the pan until it is completely melted and incorporated. Lightly season with salt and pepper, remove the thyme sprigs, then pour over the cutlets and serve immediately.

Savory French Toast with Stone Fruit and Feta Salad

Serves: 6 / **Prep Time:** 15 minutes / **Cook Time:** 15 minutes

Courtesy of Carla Hall / I think it's about time we elevate that French toast game of yours to something that you can eat any time of day, not just for breakfast on the weekends. I came up with this recipe to use up all the bread that I had in my house back when I used to travel all the time. I'd get back from a big trip and I'd always have eggs, milk, bread, and some kind of fresh herb still in my kitchen. Here I serve it with a fresh stone fruit salad. But you could serve it with tomatoes and mozzarella, or cucumbers and feta—or whatever you've got.

½ bunch dill

½ bunch parsley

2 cups arugula

4 eggs

2 cups milk

½ cup cream

2 tablespoons butter

1 loaf day-old challah, sliced into 1-inch-thick slices

FOR THE SALAD:

¼ cup extra-virgin olive oil

2 tablespoons balsamic vinegar

1 tablespoon Dijon mustard

Salt and freshly ground black pepper, to taste

3 peaches, sliced thin

1 apple, sliced thin

2 cups arugula

¼ cup mint, leaves only, chopped

½ cup feta, crumbled

1. In a blender, combine the dill, parsley, arugula, eggs, milk, and cream, and blend until smooth. Pour into a casserole dish.

2. Preheat a nonstick skillet or griddle to medium heat, then add the butter. First dip both sides of each slice of challah into the mixture, then place into the pan or on the griddle, cooking until each side is golden and crisp. Keep pieces warm in the oven until all of the slices have been cooked.

FOR THE SALAD:

3. In a large mixing bowl, add the extra-virgin olive oil, balsamic vinegar, mustard, a pinch of salt, and a grinding of pepper and whisk together. Add the peaches, apple, arugula, mint, and feta and toss to coat. Check seasonings. Serve the salad alongside the French toast.

Pan Roasted Scallops with Cauliflower, Raisins, and Pine Nuts

Serves: 4 / **Prep Time:** 10 minutes / **Cook Time:** 10 minutes

Courtesy of Michael Symon / This dish is one of my favorite easy dishes that you can make in less than twenty minutes. It's also really elegant. I think people tend to be a little intimidated by scallops, but they are so easy to make. You really just need to make sure your pan is hot, and then once you put them in the oil you don't move them until they're ready. When they are ready, they just come right up all golden brown and delicious!

2 tablespoons extra-virgin olive oil

1½ pounds scallops, abductor muscle removed (about 1 dozen)

Kosher salt and freshly ground black pepper, to taste

½ stick butter

½ cup golden raisins

4 cups small cauliflower florets

¼ cup pine nuts

1 tablespoon sherry vinegar

¼ cup parsley, chopped

1. Preheat a large cast iron skillet with olive oil over medium-high heat.

2. Pat the scallops dry on paper towels. Season with salt. Add scallops and cook without moving for 3 minutes, then flip and continue to cook on the other side, about 2 minutes. Add butter after the scallops have been cooking for 1 minute and baste the scallops with the melted butter using a spoon.

3. Once the scallops have been flipped, add raisins and cauliflower to the pan and allow to cook until cauliflower is golden brown, about 2 minutes. Season with salt and pepper. Remove from the heat and stir in the vinegar and parsley.

4. On a platter, place the scallops and top with a heaping spoonful of the cauliflower mixture.

Beef Sirloin Skewers with Soy, Ginger, and Cilantro

Serves: 18 / **Prep Time:** 5 minutes / **Cook Time:** 5 minutes

Courtesy of Michael Symon / This is a great dish for the grill because you can skewer the day before and let these meaty little bites sit overnight in the marinade. Or you can put everything together right before you fire them up and serve with some of the reserved marinade as a dipping sauce. Either way, this dish is packed with rich flavor and a great addition to any summertime table.

2 tablespoons freshly grated ginger

1 clove garlic, minced

2 ounces soy sauce

Zest and juice of 2 limes

2 tablespoons honey

2 ounces extra-virgin olive oil

3 pounds beef sirloin, cut into 1½-inch cubes

Kosher salt and freshly ground black pepper, to taste

¼ cup cilantro, roughly chopped

SPECIAL EQUIPMENT:

18 6-inch wooden skewers

1. Preheat grill to medium-high heat. Soak 18 6-inch wooden skewers in water.

2. In a large bowl or baking dish, whisk together the ginger, garlic, soy sauce, lime juice and zest, honey, and olive oil. Pour a few tablespoons into a small serving bowl and reserve.

3. Season the beef with salt and pepper. Add the seasoned beef to the soy marinade. Toss to evenly coat. Thread 2 pieces of marinated beef onto each skewer.

4. Place skewers on the preheated grill and cook for 2 minutes per side. Baste with the remaining marinade.

5. Remove the grilled beef skewers to a serving platter, garnish with cilantro, and serve with reserved marinade.

Store-Bought Solutions

Sometimes you just can't muster up the energy to figure out what to make for dinner. Hey, we get it! That's when you've just got to look to the store for assistance. There's no shame in asking for a little help from time to time. That's why we've each taken a few store-bought ingredients that you can just throw in the pot or pan with a couple of spices, and, with very little work, you'll have something on the table for your family in no time.

Clinton: When I need to whip up a dessert on the fly, I let the grocery store do the work for me and the outcome is nothing short of perfection. Well, usually. Here's a favorite: I take a prebaked pound cake from the store and brush it with a little hazelnut liqueur. Then I combine some chocolate hazelnut spread and some heavy cream and pour that mixture right over the top. Now that's a showstopping dish that took no time at all.

Mario: Want an appetizer that takes less than five minutes to prepare and zero knife skills? Take a can of garbanzo beans and drain them, then add some store-bought tapenade and a little olive oil. Toss it all together and serve over a grilled or toasted baguette. It is so flavorful I serve a version of it as an appetizer at some of my restaurants.

Carla: One of my favorite store-bought solutions is precut butternut squash. Nowadays you can get it already prepared for you in the store, and it saves a ton of time in the kitchen—peeling and chopping and deseeding. Ain't nobody got time for that! So I just sauté some onions and garlic with some curry powder before adding some chicken or vegetable stock and the cubed butternut squash. Then all you have to do is taste for seasoning, puree, and you've got a great hearty soup for lunch or dinner.

Michael: In my mind, one of the greatest time-saving ingredients you can get from the store is frozen hash browns. They're great because they come shredded, rinsed, and quickly cooked, so that all you have to do is heat them. What I like to do is take a pat of butter and a little drizzle of olive oil and add the potatoes to a nonstick sauté pan, then season with salt and pepper. Once they've browned on one side I flip and cook for another minute or two. This is a great side dish, and you can cut it up into little wedges for your guests. It feels fancy, but it takes zero effort.

Chapter 5

Seriously Simple Sweets

I'm here to tell you that you don't have to be a pastry chef to whip up some deliciously decadent desserts. You just need a quick trip to the grocery store, a plan, and a little creativity.

Between broken crusts and undercooked centers, baking can be tough. For those of you who consider yourselves more of a cook than a baker, you're not alone. I am right there with you. That's why, when I find myself in search of the perfect sweet treat to whip up for my friends and family (one that will keep the whole group satisfied), I just keep it simple.

We've got plenty of chocolaty, creamy, fruity, and oh-so-oozy dishes in this chapter that will give you all the tools you need to win the respect of your guests and the title of Dessert Diva. There are some four-ingredient indulgences and there are cakes that you can make in the microwave. That's right, I said microwave! There are sweet treats that will take your brunch game to a whole new level, and, of course, chocolate! Did I mention chocolate? So please, sit back, relax, and enjoy the sugar rush. *The Chew* crew's got you covered!

—MARIO BATALI

Churro Waffles

Serves: 8 / **Prep Time:** 10 minutes / **Cook Time:** 10 minutes

Courtesy of Carla Hall / I went through a phase on the show where I tried to "waffle" everything—and I mean everything! Biscuits and gravy waffles, falafel waffles . . . but my favorite kind of waffle by far was this churro waffle. I loved it so much; it was so perfectly crispy and sweet and covered in gooey chocolate that I just had to share it with you. I feel like this dish can be served at a really decadent brunch or a casual family gathering. This crunchy waffle, tossed in cinnamon and sugar and then covered in chocolate sauce, is a true recipe for success.

1 cup all-purpose flour

1 tablespoon, plus 1 teaspoon, ground cinnamon, divided

1 teaspoon ground nutmeg

1 teaspoon ground ginger

½ teaspoon ground allspice

1 cup granulated sugar

½ cup unsalted butter

1 cup water

1 teaspoon salt

3 eggs at room temperature

Store-bought chocolate sauce, to serve

1. In a large bowl, whisk the flour, 1 teaspoon cinnamon, nutmeg, ginger, and allspice. Set aside. In a small bowl, combine the sugar and remaining cinnamon.

2. Place the butter and water in a medium saucepan and bring to a simmer. Remove from the heat, add in the flour mixture, and stir until the mixture pulls away from the sides of the pan, about 2 minutes. Add the eggs, 1 at a time, and make sure that each egg is fully incorporated before adding the next.

3. Heat a waffle iron.

4. Spray the preheated waffle iron with cooking spray. Ladle churro batter onto the waffle iron and close to cook until the churro waffles are golden and crispy. Remove from the waffle iron, sprinkle with cinnamon sugar, and set aside. Continue making churro waffles with the remaining batter.

5. Drizzle the finished churro waffles with chocolate sauce.

Chocolate Hazelnut S'mores Dip

Serves: 6–8 / **Prep Time:** 10 minutes / **Cook Time:** 3 minutes

Courtesy of Michael Symon / When I was a kid, s'mores were my favorite dessert. I loved making those sweet little sandwiches on camping trips with my family. For me there was an art to the perfect s'more. Now I live in New York, so I understand very well that not everyone has access to a campfire or even a fireplace. That's why I created this recipe, so that you can relive those childhood memories no matter where you live. The best part: it's incredibly easy and it feeds a crowd!

1 cup mascarpone

1 cup chocolate hazelnut spread

½ cup heavy cream

¼ teaspoon kosher salt

1 cup marshmallow cream

Flaky sea salt, to garnish

Graham crackers, to serve

Bananas, peeled, sliced, to serve

Pretzels, to serve

Potato chips, to serve

1. In the bowl of a food processor, add the mascarpone and chocolate hazelnut spread, and blend until combined. Scrape the sides, add the cream and salt, and blend until smooth. Divide the mascarpone mixture into 6 ramekins.

2. Fill a piping bag with the marshmallow cream, and pipe a thin layer on top of the mascarpone mixture. Using a kitchen torch, or under the broiler, caramelize the tops until golden brown, about 2 minutes. Garnish with flaky sea salt. Serve with graham crackers, bananas, pretzels, and potato chips for dipping.

Affogato Milk Shake

Serves: 2 / **Prep Time:** 5 minutes / **Cook Time:** 1 minute

Courtesy of Mario Batali / I think that in an affogato, the Italians have created the simplest dessert of all cultures. It's basically a scoop of gelato and some warm espresso. The perfect balance of hot and cold, bitter and sweet. Here we've taken that idea to the next level by turning it into an indulgent milk shake. It may not be traditional, but baby you can't deny it's delicious.

1 pint vanilla gelato

½ cup milk

½ cup espresso, cooled

2 teaspoons cocoa powder

In the carafe of a blender, add the gelato and milk and blend to combine. Pour into two glasses. Divide the espresso between the two glasses and dust with cocoa powder over the top.

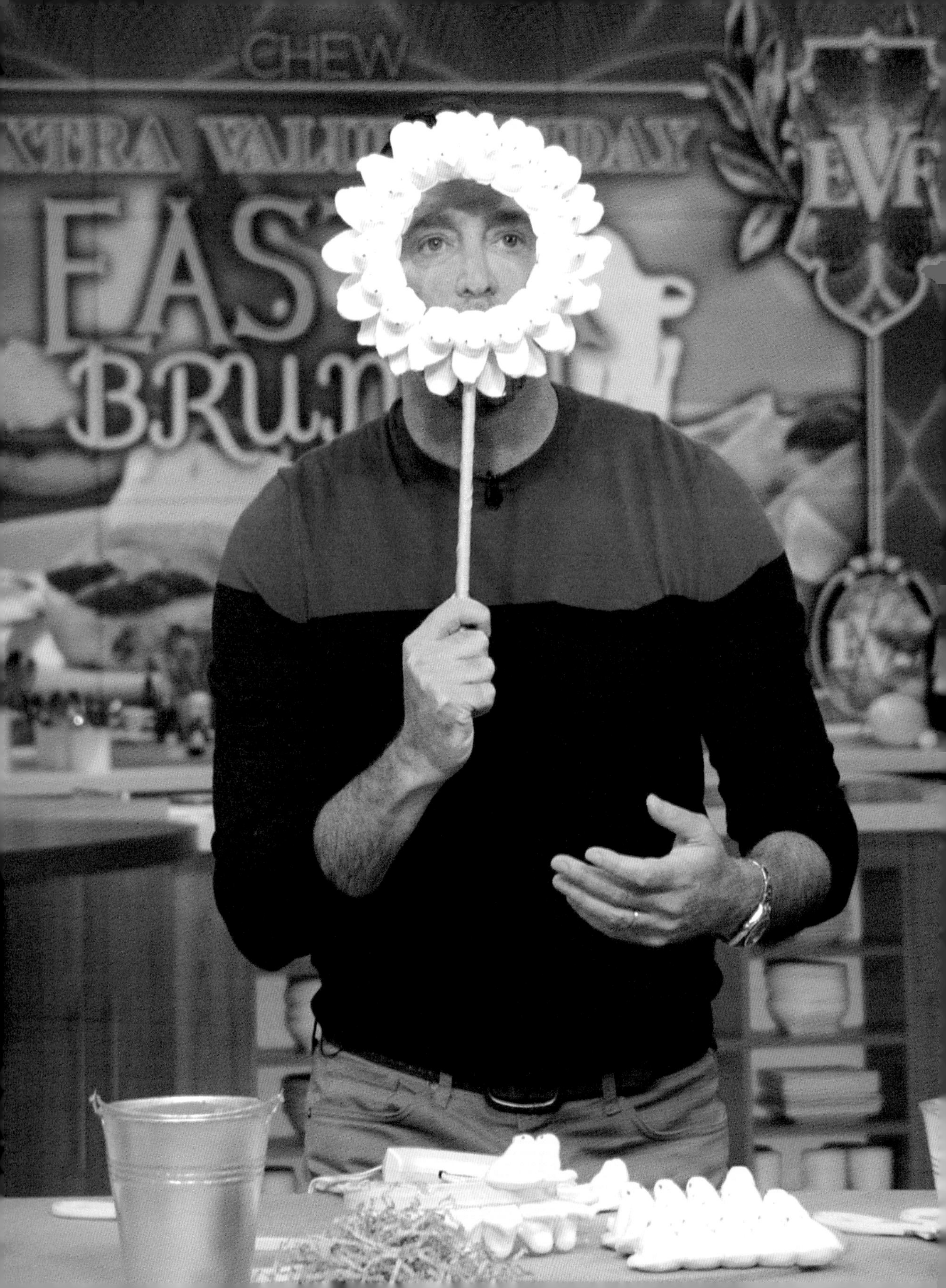
CHEW

Spiced Apples with Cream

Serves: 4 / **Prep Time:** 5 minutes / **Cook Time:** 15 minutes

Courtesy of Clinton Kelly / I like to think of this dish as sort of a deconstructed apple pie. You've got apples stewed in all of those delicious pie spices, and then you top those with a whipped cream that you cover with crushed-up cookies that mimic the crunch of piecrust. This is perfect for those of you who feel like you might not be up to the challenge of a full-on pie, and it comes together so quickly that it's great for a last-minute dinner party. It's the perfect dish to ease your way into fall.

2 tablespoons butter

4 Granny Smith apples, peeled, cored, cut into ¼-inch-thick wedges

¼ cup light brown sugar

1 cinnamon stick

1 whole nutmeg

1 container whipped cream cheese

⅓ cup sour cream

1–2 tablespoons heavy cream

2 cups vanilla wafers, crushed

1. In a large sauté pan, add butter and melt over medium heat. Add apples and allow to cook until slightly soft, about 4 minutes. Add brown sugar and stir to combine. Using a Microplane, grate 1 teaspoon fresh cinnamon and ½ teaspoon fresh nutmeg and mix to combine. Cook until apples have broken down, another 5 minutes.

2. In a medium bowl, add the cream cheese, sour cream, and heavy cream and fold to combine.

3. Divide the apples between bowls, then top with crushed vanilla wafers and cream cheese mixture.

Sugared Plums with Crème Fraîche and Amaretti Cookies

Serves: 6 / **Prep Time:** 5 minutes / **Cook Time:** 5 minutes

Courtesy of Carla Hall / I'd like you to take a minute to count how many ingredients are in this dish . . . that's right, one, two, three, four! Yes, four ingredients, and this dish takes just minutes to make. How awesome is that? The flavors touch on all of the elements that make a great bite of dessert: sweet, crunchy, creamy, and tart. Whip this dish up at your next get-together and your friends will be truly impressed by your greatness.

3 ripe plums, halved and pitted

3 tablespoons, plus 1 teaspoon sugar

1 cup crushed amaretti cookies

6 tablespoons crème fraîche

1. Preheat broiler.

2. Arrange the plums, cut-side up, on a baking sheet and sprinkle with the sugar.

3. Broil until tops begin to brown and caramelize, about 2 minutes. Do not leave unattended as they will brown quickly.

4. Sprinkle the plums with crushed amaretti cookies and dollop the plums with the crème fraîche to serve.

Banana Bread Pudding

Serves: 10 / **Prep Time:** 20 minutes / **Cook Time:** 1 hour, 30 minutes

Courtesy of Michael Symon / What happens when you combine banana pudding and brunch together into one magical dish? Pure bliss. I think this dish is perfect for a baby shower or brunch to celebrate something really special because it's mostly a dessert, though it feels a little like breakfast because there are croissants in it. That's the greatest excuse ever to have dessert for breakfast, if you ask me.

1 tablespoon softened butter

3 large eggs

3 large egg yolks

2½ cups half-and-half

2 cups whole milk

1 cup sugar

1½ teaspoons vanilla extract

1 pinch salt

½ teaspoon freshly grated nutmeg

6 croissants, preferably day-old, sliced in half crosswise

2 cups sliced bananas

FOR THE CHOCOLATE SAUCE:

1 cup heavy cream

¼ cup sugar

Pinch salt

4 ounces semisweet chocolate, chopped

1 tablespoon unsweetened cocoa powder

1. Preheat your oven to 350°F. Grease a 9 x 13 baking dish with the softened butter and set aside.

2. In a large mixing bowl, whisk together the eggs, yolks, half-and-half, milk, sugar, vanilla, salt, and nutmeg until smooth.

3. Place the bottom halves of the croissants in the prepared pan. Add the bananas in an even layer. Place the top halves of the croissants on top. Pour the custard over the top, press down slightly, and let soak for at least 10 minutes. Cover the pan with foil, tented with a few holes poked, and bake for 45 minutes.

4. Uncover, then bake for another 40 minutes until the custard is set. Remove from the oven to cool slightly. Drizzle warm chocolate sauce over the banana bread pudding to serve.

FOR THE CHOCOLATE SAUCE:

5. Add the cream, sugar, and salt to a medium saucepan and place over medium heat. Bring the cream to a simmer, stirring constantly, until the sugar dissolves. Add the chocolate and cocoa powder, whisking constantly to melt and combine chocolate.

Olive Oil and Orange Cake

Serves: 8 / **Prep Time:** 15 minutes / **Cook Time:** 50 minutes

Courtesy of Mario Batali / Close your eyes and picture a sun-soaked orange grove in Sicily: warm and breezy, endless fields, and sunshine smiles. Now imagine just what that would taste like. Well, like my delicious orange and olive oil cake, of course! If you've got olive oil, oranges, and sugar at your house, then you've got dessert on the table tonight, my friends.

6 medium oranges

½ cup extra-virgin olive oil

4 large eggs

½ teaspoon salt

1 cup sugar

2¼ cups all-purpose flour

2 tablespoons baking powder

FOR THE ICING:

1½ cups powdered sugar

Zest of 1 lime, plus 3 tablespoons lime juice

1. Preheat the oven to 350°F. Oil a 9-inch-round cake pan.

2. Using a grater, zest all the oranges, and juice one of the oranges. (Reserve the fruit for another use.) In a small bowl, combine the orange zest, juice, and olive oil. Set aside.

3. In a large bowl, with an electric mixer, beat the eggs and salt until frothy and light, about 2 minutes. Slowly beat in the sugar, and continue to mix until pale and thick, about 2 minutes more.

4. Combine flour and baking powder, and gradually beat into the egg mixture. Fold in the orange zest mixture just until incorporated.

5. Pour the batter into the prepared pan. Bake for 50 minutes, or until a toothpick inserted in the center of the cake comes out clean. Cool on a rack for 10 minutes, then remove from the pan and cool to room temperature.

FOR THE ICING:

6. Whisk together the powdered sugar and lime juice and zest in a large bowl. Drizzle over the top of the cooled cake. Slice and serve.

Peaches and Cream No-Bake Cheesecake

Serves: 12 / **Prep Time:** 5 minutes / **Inactive Time:** 4 hours

Courtesy of Clinton Kelly / Summer is all about simple and delicious meals, and the last thing you want when it's really hot outside is to sit in an even hotter kitchen waiting for the dessert to finish in the oven. So here I've created a no-bake masterpiece that will have your friends calling you the five-minute gourmet.

2 cups graham cracker crumbs

6 tablespoons unsalted butter, melted

8 ounces cream cheese, room temperature

1 14.5-ounce can sweetened condensed milk

1 16-ounce bag frozen peaches

1. Spray a loaf pan with nonstick spray. Line the pan with parchment paper so it hangs over the edges, creating handles. Spray the parchment with more nonstick spray.

2. In a medium bowl, combine the graham cracker crumbs and butter. Press into the bottom of the prepared loaf pan.

3. In a large bowl, whisk together the cream cheese and sweetened condensed milk. Fold in the frozen peaches. Pour the peach mixture over the graham cracker crust. Spread the top out into an even layer. Place in the freezer for 4 hours or overnight. Remove from freezer 15 minutes before serving.

4. To serve, cut cheesecake into slices.

Mexican Chocolate Blender Flan

Serves: 6 / **Prep Time:** 20 minutes / **Inactive Time:** 1 hour / **Cook Time:** 25–30 minutes

Courtesy of Carla Hall / The gloriously rich, velvety custard known as flan is one of those classic dishes that you see on restaurant menus all the time that seems to be really fancy and very hard to make, right? Well, I've created this blender version that saves you time and cleanup. No bowl, no whisk, no problem!

¾ cup granulated sugar

3 ounces bittersweet chocolate chips, melted

7 ounces sweetened condensed milk

1 cup whole milk

3 large eggs, room temperature

1 teaspoon vanilla extract

½ teaspoon ground cinnamon

¼ teaspoon ground cayenne

½ teaspoon kosher salt

2 ounces bittersweet chocolate, shaved, for garnish

1. Preheat oven to 325°F. Place 6 (6-ounce) ramekins inside a roasting pan. Spray ramekins with nonstick cooking spray. Fill a kettle with water and bring to a boil.

2. In a small saucepan, add ¾ cup of sugar and 2 tablespoons of water. Bring to a boil, then reduce heat to a simmer. Cook until the caramel turns golden, without stirring. Swirl the caramel around in the pan to ensure even cooking. Immediately divide caramel into prepared ramekins.

3. In the carafe of a blender, add melted chocolate, sweetened condensed milk, whole milk, eggs, vanilla, cinnamon, cayenne, and salt. Blend until smooth. Do not overmix. Divide the mixture among the caramel-coated ramekins. Pouring around the ramekins, fill the roasting pan with enough water to come halfway up the ramekins. Carefully place in the oven and bake for 25–30 minutes, until custard has a slight jiggle in the center. Remove from the oven and allow to cool in the water for 10 minutes.

4. Remove from water and dry ramekins. Place in the refrigerator to cool for at least 1 hour.

5. To serve, loosen flan with a paring knife that you run around the edges of the ramekin. Flip each onto a plate, topping with any caramel left in the ramekin. Garnish with shaved chocolate.

Salted Bourbon Caramel Apples

Serves: 10 / **Prep Time:** 10 minutes / **Cook Time:** 45 minutes

Courtesy of Michael Symon / This is one of the easiest candied-apple recipes that you'll ever come across. It's basically dump, stir, and simmer. I put bourbon in mine and then cover it with sea salt for an adult version. But if you want to make them a little more kid friendly for Halloween, feel free to replace the bourbon with apple cider and top with pretzels.

1 box dark brown sugar

1 cup unsalted butter, room temperature

1 14-ounce can sweetened condensed milk

⅔ cup honey

⅓ cup pure maple syrup

1 teaspoon vanilla extract

2 teaspoons Maldon sea salt

2 tablespoons bourbon whiskey or apple cider

10 Granny Smith apples

10 skewers

1. Combine first 6 ingredients in a heavy-bottomed 4-quart saucepan. Stir with a wooden spoon over medium-low heat until sugar dissolves (no crystals are left when caramel is rubbed between fingers), occasionally brushing down sides of pan with a wet pastry brush.

2. Attach clip-on candy thermometer to the side of the pan. Increase heat to medium-high; cook the caramel at a rolling boil until the thermometer registers 236°F. Remove from heat and stir in bourbon. Cool for about 5 minutes.

3. Bring a pot of water to a boil and briefly dunk each apple into the water. Rub the wax off (if the apples are store-bought) with a clean towel.

4. Remove the stems from the apples and push in the skewers. While caramel cools, line 2 sheet trays with greased parchment or waxed paper.

5. Dip one apple at a time into the caramel, submerging all but the very top. Lift the apple out, allowing excess caramel to drip back into the pan. Turn the apple caramel-side up and hold for several seconds to help set caramel around the apple. Garnish caramel apple with Maldon sea salt. Place the coated apple on a prepared sheet tray. Repeat with remaining apples, caramel, and salt, spacing apples apart as caramel will pool a bit.

220

The Chew: Quick & Easy

Pastelitos

Courtesy of Mario Batali / These are a version of one of my favorite Cuban pastries that I love to get from those little stands on the streets and even on the beach in Miami. They are so easy to put together and they freeze incredibly well. You just need some cream cheese, guava paste, and store-bought puff pastry. Now if you can't find the guava, apricot jam works just as well. Either way, these are the perfect sweet afternoon treats to enjoy with coffee, preferably Cuban style.

1 package store-bought puff pastry, thawed

2 eggs, plus 1 tablespoon water whisked together

1 package guava paste

4 ounces cream cheese, softened

1 teaspoon lemon juice

2 tablespoons sugar

1 tablespoon milk

⅛ teaspoon salt

1. Preheat oven to 350°F.

2. Lightly roll out puff pastry on a floured surface. Cut into 2½- to 3-inch squares.

3. Lightly grease a mini-muffin tin with nonstick cooking spray. Press a square of puff pastry into each cup with the edges sticking out. Set aside.

4. In a medium mixing bowl, combine the cream cheese, lemon juice, sugar, milk, and salt. Stir until smooth.

5. Place a teaspoon of guava paste into the center of each puff pastry cup. Top with a dollop of cream cheese mixture. Bake for 20–25 minutes, or until golden brown and crispy. Remove and allow to cool before serving.

Cinnamon-Sugar Casserole

Serves: 12 / **Prep Time:** 10 minutes / **Cook Time:** 20–25 minutes

Courtesy of Clinton Kelly / As a home cook, I am always trying to test the limits of using store-bought ingredients in my desserts. I want to make my life easier, but I don't want to sacrifice quality and flavor. The main ingredient in this dish is store-bought dinner rolls. I know, maybe I took it too far, but it is so delicious you won't believe it. I take a whole package of dinner rolls and cut them in half, and then I make a giant cinnamon-sugar sandwich, dip that in custard, and bake it in the oven. It's crazy good.

FOR THE TOPPING:

4 tablespoons unsalted butter, room temperature

¼ cup light brown sugar

1 teaspoon ground cinnamon

½ cup pecans, roughly chopped

2 tablespoons flour

¼ cup rolled oats

FOR THE CASSEROLE:

1 package sweet Hawaiian dinner rolls

2 tablespoons butter, for greasing dish

8 ounces cream cheese, room temperature

¼ cup light brown sugar

1½ cups pecans, roughly chopped

1 tablespoon ground cinnamon

FOR THE CUSTARD:

4 eggs

1 cup milk

½ cup cream

1 teaspoon vanilla extract

1 pinch salt

Powdered sugar, to garnish

FOR THE TOPPING:

1. Combine all the ingredients in a small mixing bowl until crumbly. Set aside.

FOR THE CASSEROLE:

2. Preheat oven to 350°F.

3. Grease the inside of a 9 x 9 baking dish.

4. Remove the top of the rolls from the bottom of the rolls, keeping the top rolls connected and the bottom rolls connected. Place the top buns upside down on a baking sheet. Place the bottom rolls on a separate baking sheet. Place the rolls in the oven to toast, about 5 minutes. Remove and set aside to cool.

5. In a medium bowl, mix together cream cheese, light brown sugar, pecans, and ground cinnamon.

6. Spread the cream cheese mixture in an even layer on top of the bottom rolls. Top with the toasted top rolls. Pull each roll off, creating individual sandwiches.

FOR THE CUSTARD:

7. In a large bowl, add the eggs, milk, cream, vanilla extract, and a pinch of salt. Whisk well to combine. Dip each roll into the custard. Shingle the rolls into the baking dish. Crumble the topping on top.

8. Bake in oven for 20–25 minutes. Remove and allow to cool for 10 minutes before serving. Garnish with a sprinkle of powdered sugar.

Jeweled Citrus Bark

Serves: 10–12 / **Prep Time:** 5 minutes / **Inactive Time:** 1 hour / **Cook Time:** 5 minutes

Courtesy of Carla Hall / In my opinion, the holidays are the most delicious time of the year. And when I give a gift around Christmastime, I give food because it satisfies the soul and brings everyone together around the table. This DIY gift is just as easy to put together as it is tasty, and it makes the perfect stocking stuffer! Go ahead and play with flavor combinations like peppermint and chocolate, or even pretzels and chocolate. The possibilities are endless.

3 cups bittersweet chocolate, melted

2 teaspoons coarse sea salt

3 cups white chocolate, melted

½ cup candied orange zest

½ cup dried cherries

½ cup pistachios, shelled and toasted

1. In a medium microwave safe bowl, add the bittersweet chocolate and place in the microwave for 30 seconds. Give it a stir and return to the microwave for another 30 seconds, or until chocolate is melted and glossy.

2. Pour the melted bittersweet chocolate onto a parchment-lined baking sheet, sprinkle with coarse sea salt, then let the chocolate harden slightly.

3. In another medium microwave safe bowl, add the white chocolate and place in the microwave for 30 seconds. Give it a stir and return to the microwave for another 30 seconds, or until the chocolate is melted and glossy.

4. Pour the melted white chocolate over the bittersweet chocolate. Using a toothpick, swirl the 2 chocolates to make a marble pattern. Sprinkle the candied orange zest, dried cherries, and pistachios all over the white chocolate. Allow the bark to set for at least an hour.

5. Break apart the bark with your hands.

Microwave Carrot Cake

Serves: 2 / **Prep Time:** 5 minutes / **Cook Time:** 2 minutes

Courtesy of Michael Symon / I am a huge fan of the microwave cake. I've made them in competitions on the shows *Iron Chef* and *Chopped*, and in both competitions these dishes helped me take home the trophy. Now this is just a basic carrot cake recipe that I divided into mugs and baked in just under ninety seconds. I like to call these my carrot "cup" cakes for obvious reasons. No matter what you call them, you can't deny the fact that they are truly delicious.

1 egg, separated

6 tablespoons pastry flour

1 carrot, grated

3 tablespoons brown sugar

¼ teaspoon baking soda

2 tablespoons extra-virgin olive oil

2 ounces buttermilk

2 tablespoons toasted pecans, crushed

2 tablespoons golden raisins

⅛ teaspoon nutmeg

⅛ teaspoon cinnamon, plus more to garnish

Zest of 1 orange

Sour cream, to garnish

1. In a small bowl, whip egg white until soft and fluffy.

2. In another small mixing bowl, mix egg yolk, pastry flour, grated carrot, brown sugar, baking soda, olive oil, buttermilk, toasted pecans, raisins, nutmeg, cinnamon, orange zest, and egg whites. Combine until all ingredients are just incorporated.

3. Divide between 2 mugs and microwave on high for 2–2½ minutes.

4. Garnish with sour cream and cinnamon and serve.

Apple Brown Betty

Serves: 8 / **Prep Time:** 15 minutes / **Cook Time:** 40 minutes

Courtesy of Mario Batali / This is my kind of dessert. You cut up some apples and toss them with some lemon juice and some toasted biscuits. Next you bathe them in a whole lot of melted butter, toss in sugar and spices, and then just throw it in a baking dish. You don't have to be Betty Crocker to make this delicious brown Betty. It's so easy even a child could pull this one off. In fact, I used to make it with my boys all the time when they were kids. Make sure you serve it warm with lots of ice cream. My mouth is watering just thinking about it.

6 medium Empire apples

½ lemon, juice and zest

4 cups cubed day-old, store-bought biscuits, bread, or cake

½ cup butter

½ cup packed brown sugar

¼ teaspoon ground nutmeg, preferably freshly grated

Pinch cloves

Vanilla ice cream, for serving

1. Preheat the oven to 300°F.

2. Peel and core the apples and cut them into ¾-inch slices. Transfer to a large bowl, then zest the lemon and squeeze the juice over the apple slices and toss gently to cover the apples and keep them from browning before baking. Set aside.

3. On a 12 x 17 baking sheet, arrange the biscuit cubes or bread in one layer and bake on the center rack of the oven until lightly brown, about 10 minutes.

4. Meanwhile, melt the butter in a small saucepan. When the biscuit cubes are done, transfer them to a large bowl, pour in half of the melted butter, and toss together. Set aside.

5. Add the brown sugar, nutmeg, and cloves to the apples and gently toss together.

6. Raise the oven temperature to 375°F. Place ⅓ of the toasted biscuit cubes on the bottom of a 9-inch-square baking dish. Top with half the apple slices. Top with another ⅓ of the biscuit cubes and then the remaining apples. Top the apples with the remaining biscuit cubes. Pour the remaining butter over everything. Bake on the center rack for 30 minutes, until the top is nicely browned.

7. Remove from the heat and serve warm with vanilla ice cream. Brown Betty is best made the same day you are going to serve it, as once you cover and store it, it loses its consistency.

Rustic Berry Tart

Serves: 8 / **Prep Time:** 10 minutes / **Cook Time:** 30 minutes

Courtesy of Clinton Kelly / This rustic berry tart is so visually authentic that it will look like it came right from the glossy pages of a magazine or the Pinterest board of your favorite pastry chef. A tart from scratch would cost three hours of your day, but if you make my store-bought version, you'll save at least two and a half of those hours. That means time for a mani-pedi and a couple episodes of *Judge Judy*! You're welcome!

1 store-bought pie shell, thawed

1 12-ounce bag frozen mixed berries, thawed and drained

½ cup sugar

2 tablespoons cornstarch

1 tablespoon lemon zest

Pinch salt

1 egg, lightly beaten, with 1 teaspoon of water

1. Preheat oven to 375°F.

2. Remove the thawed pie shell from the tin and place in the middle of a parchment-lined baking sheet.

3. In a large mixing bowl, add berries, sugar, cornstarch, lemon zest, and salt. Gently fold together to combine.

4. Pile the berry mixture onto the center of the pie dough, leaving a 2-inch border. Gently fold over the border toward the center, pleating as you go around the tart. Brush the border with the egg wash.

5. Place in the oven and bake for 30 minutes, until the crust is golden and the fruit in the center is bubbly. Remove from the oven and allow to cool 10 minutes before serving.

Pineapple-Lime Sorbet

Serves: 4 / **Prep Time:** 1 minute

Courtesy of Carla Hall / I live in a tiny apartment in New York City, and I definitely don't have room in my kitchen for an ice cream machine. Who wants to clean up all of that mess anyway? Not me. That's why I created this amazing and refreshing pineapple and lime sorbet that you can make in your blender. No expensive or fancy equipment is required. On a hot summer day, there is nothing more refreshing than these flavors.

2 cups frozen pineapple chunks

Zest and juice of 2 limes

¼ cup cold water

Sugar or coconut water, if needed

1. Combine all of the ingredients in a blender and puree until mixture resembles sorbet. Serve immediately or place in a covered container and freeze until ready to eat. Garnish with more lime zest if desired.

2. If your pineapple is not so sweet, add some sugar or coconut water.

Pear Tarte Tatin

Serves: 10–12 / **Prep Time:** 5 minutes / **Cook Time:** 35 minutes

Courtesy of Mario Batali / I think this may be the world's easiest dessert, and it is certainly the most impressive. There is no dessert that can wow a crowd better than a tarte tatin. Whether you're using the classic apple version or switching it up with my pear treat, there is no greater moment at a dinner party than the fantastic reveal of this dessert. Once you've cooked up the caramel sauce, nestled those pears in the pan, and tucked them in ever so slightly with dough, set them in the oven for just a few minutes. And when it's ready to serve, just flip it over table-side, revealing a beautifully displayed arrangement of deliciousness.

4 tablespoons butter

½ cup sugar

2 or 3 pods cardamom

1 teaspoon salt

4 pears, peeled, cored, quartered lengthwise

1 tablespoon brandy

1 sheet puff pastry, thawed

All-purpose flour, for dusting

Vanilla ice cream, to serve

1. Preheat oven to 375°F.

2. In a large ovenproof nonstick sauté pan, melt butter over medium-high heat. Once bubbling, add the sugar, then allow to brown on medium-low heat for about 5 minutes. Add cardamom pods and stir in the salt. Add pears to pan cut-side down. Cook until the pears begin to caramelize and flip pears. Arrange pears in a circle. Remove from heat, pour in brandy, and ignite using a lighter. Allow flame to extinguish.

3. On a lightly floured surface, roll the puff pastry out to ¼-inch thick. Top the pears with puff pastry and tuck the edges in. Transfer to a preheated oven and cook for 15–20 minutes, or until pastry is golden brown.

4. Place a platter that is larger than the pan over the top of the pan and carefully flip the platter and pan to reveal the tarte. Serve with ice cream.

Lemon Curd and Berry Crepes

Serves: 4 / **Prep Time:** 15 minutes / **Cook Time:** 10 minutes

Courtesy of Michael Symon / This recipe is the perfect marriage of store-bought ingredients mixed with homemade goodness. When you're just starting out in the world of baking, it's important to try new techniques, but also to know your limitations. So when I was starting out, I would combine something homemade and something store-bought because I knew if the homemade wasn't perfect, the store-bought would save the day. That's what I've done here with this recipe. The homemade crepes combined with store-bought lemon curd and some fresh berries give you something elegant and delicious that everyone will love.

2 eggs

¾ cup milk

½ cup water

1 cup flour

3 tablespoons butter, melted

1 cup store-bought lemon curd

1½ cups whipped cream, plus more for garnish

3 tablespoons sweetened shredded coconut

¼ cup powdered sugar

Zest of 1 orange

Butter, for pan

Berries, to garnish

1. Combine the eggs, milk, and water and whisk in the flour and melted butter. Let it rest while you prepare the crepe filling.

2. In a bowl, mix together the lemon curd, whipped cream, coconut, powdered sugar, and orange zest.

3. In a small nonstick pan over medium-heat, melt butter just to coat pan. Add a small ladle of the crepe batter and carefully swirl pan quickly to coat bottom. Cook on first side for 30 seconds, and then flip and cook another 20–30 seconds. Transfer to a board and continue to make your crepes. Spoon some of the filling into the center of each crepe in a line and then fold sides over top. Garnish with berries and whipped cream.

Crispy Peanut Butter Balls

Serves: 24 / **Prep Time:** 20 minutes / **Cook Time:** 15 minutes

Courtesy of Clinton Kelly / This is one of those recipe ideas that you come up with late at night when you're just about to drift off to sleep. You know, the kind you force yourself to write down so that you'll remember in the morning? Well, half the time I wake up and read the notes I have written to myself and can't quite understand why I thought it was such a good idea in the first place. But when I woke up one morning to find the recipe for this tasty little morsel scratched on a sticky note next to my bed, I was totally reminded of what a genius I am!

2 cups creamy peanut butter

1 stick butter

½ teaspoon salt

2 cups powdered sugar

2 cups puffed rice cereal

12 ounces semisweet chocolate chips, melted

1. In a small saucepot, melt peanut butter and butter. Remove from heat and stir in salt. Set aside.

2. In a large bowl, stir together powdered sugar and rice cereal.

3. Add the wet ingredients into the dry ingredients, then stir until combined. Using a small scoop, roll mixture into balls and place on a parchment-lined cookie sheet. Place in refrigerator until firm, about 15 minutes.

4. Meanwhile, melt chocolate over a double boiler. Remove peanut butter balls from refrigerator and dip into melted chocolate. Allow chocolate to set, about 10 minutes in the refrigerator.

Dessert Fixes in a Pinch!

The hardest part of baking is knowing that once you've whisked all your ingredients together, rolled out all the dough, or toasted all the nuts, you've still got to actually bake that dessert into something edible. Once you shut the oven door, you just have to say a little prayer or cross your fingers and leave it to the cooking/baking gods because at that point, it's out of your hands. So we've given you some foolproof tips to help you turn even the worst baking disaster into something delicious . . . just in case!

Carla Hall: Did you forget to put your carton of ice cream in the freezer when you were unpacking the groceries? We've all done it. Don't throw it away, and don't you even think about trying to refreeze that carton, hoping no one will notice. Just combine one pint of melted ice cream with one and a half cups of self-rising flour and a little cinnamon. Then bake at 350°F for fifteen minutes. You know what you'll have just in time for breakfast? Biscuits!

Clinton Kelly: Have you ever pulled out that tray of brownies only to find that your oven was set too high? Or perhaps your timer had been going off for the past half hour, but you couldn't hear it over the Olivia Newton-John's greatest hits music you were blasting. Well, I'll tell you I've been there. So here's what you do: cut those dried-out little brownies into cubes and place a couple in a wineglass. Then you top with a few drops of amaretto or Frangelico, and whipped cream, and repeat until the glass is full. Chill in the refrigerator for about ten minutes and you've got a moist and delicious brownie trifle ready to go.

Mario Batali: Does this happen to you? You take your pound cake out of the oven and it's beautiful—the top is slightly cracked like a good pound cake should be, and it just looks like an Instagram photo. But then you cut into it, and it's not raw but maybe just a little gummy. Not

the worst thing, but it's happened to me a few more times than I'd like to admit. So I came up with a solution that I think tastes better than the original. Cut the pound cake into slices and slather them with a little butter on both sides. Then add them to a hot nonstick pan and cook them until they are crispy on both sides. Top with sour cream and some fresh berries. It's perfect for breakfast or dessert!

Michael Symon: Cakes have not always been my thing, so I've had a lot of practice turning a poorly baked cake into something else. We've all had a cake-baking disaster like this: your cake looks great in the oven, puffed into a gorgeous dome, but then you take it out to cool, come back ten minutes later, and all the air has left and you've got a sunken cavern. Well, here's a great solution: scoop out a little of the center and then heat up some honey, orange juice, and a little water. Next, pour it all over the cake and let it soak up all of that syrup. Then fill the hole in the center with figs or stone fruit and whipped cream and a shower of powdered sugar. No one will ever know that there's a hole in the center of that cake.

French Toast Roll-Up courtesy of
Clinton Kelly, recipe on page 15.

Index

Note: Italic page numbers refer
to illustrations.

A

Affogato Milk Shake, 2, *202, 203*
Ajo Verde, 161
Alsatian Tarte Flambé, 118, *119*
Appetizers
  Ajo Verde, 161
  Alsatian Tarte Flambé, 118,
    119
  Baked Beef Sliders, 114
  Chicken and Shrimp
    Dumplings, 117
  Curry Chicken Salad, 20
  Feta and Dill Tiropita, 112
  Franks 'n' Beans in a Blanket,
    183
  Grilled Lemon Oregano
    Chicken Wings, 27
  Ham and Cheese Puff Pastry
    Pinwheels, 107
  Mozzarella Sticks, 26
  Prosciutto with Baked, Stuffed
    Figs, 110, *111*
  Quesadilla Party, 122
  Salami Cornucopia, 113
  Slow Cooker Spicy Eggplant
    Sauce, 81
  Swiss Chard and Ricotta Pizza
    Poppers, 24, *25*

Apples
  Apple Brown Betty, 229
  Apple Cider Syrup, 153
  Apple Pancake Rings with
    Apple Cider Syrup, 153
  Brie and Apple Grilled
    Cheese, 162, *163*
  Salted Bourbon Caramel
    Apples, 220
  Spiced Apples with Cream,
    207
Arroz con Pollo, 88, *89*
Arugula, *Zucchini Spaghetti*
  with Arugula Pesto, 169
Asian Barbecue Sauce, 62

B

Bagel Stuffing, 46, *47*
Baked Beef Sliders, 114
Bananas, *Banana Bread*
  Pudding, 213
Batali, Mario
  Affogato Milk Shake, 2, *202,*
    203
  Ajo Verde, 161
  Alsatian Tarte Flambé, 118,
    119
  Apple Brown Betty, 229
  Arroz con Pollo, 88, *89*
  Black Bean and Egg Tacos,
    154

  Braised Chicken with Potatoes
    and Tarragon, 91
  Calamari Sicilian Lifeguard
    Style, 174
  Chicken Under a Brick, 39
  Chilaquiles, 16, *17*
  Colorado Green Chili with
    Chicken, 76, *77*
  on dessert fixes, 242–243
  on desserts, 196
  on entertaining in an instant,
    148
  Molasses-Glazed Ham with
    Honey Butter, 51
  Olive Oil and Orange Cake,
    214, *215*
  Pasta e Fagioli (Pasta and
    Bean Soup), 64
  Pastelitos, 221
  Pear Tarte Tatin, 236, *237*
  Perfect Roasted Chicken, 131
  Prosciutto with Baked, Stuffed
    Figs, 110, *111*
  Quick Steak au Poivre, 180,
    181
  Red Wine Braised Brisket,
    142, *143*
  Sausage and Pepper Hero,
    165
  on sheet-pan dinners, 100
  Shrimp in Acqua Pazzo, 36, *37*

The Chew: Quick & Easy